Table of Contents

An Era In Time...7
Application of Responsibility 9
Art of Growing 10
At The Living Edge 12
Balance and Purpose 13
Behind the Scene...15
Blind Moments...16
Consider The End 18
Creative Power Within 20
Courtship 21
Cycle of Years..23
David and King Saul 24
Deception 26
Element of Time 28
Era of Abundance...29
Events in History...31
"Except a Man is Born. . ." 33
Free Spirit...35
Final Notice..36
Florence Nightingale 38
For Whom Do We Work?...40
Friends...42
From Out of the Past...43
George Washington 45
Guarantee..47
Guiding Light...49
Happiness at Home..50

Helen Keller 52
Hesitation 55
If 56
In Review 58
It Begins and Ends With You 59
Journey of Trust 61
Judgment Day 62
Law 64
Life In Motion 66
Living Among Us 67
Making the Most 69
Measuring Rod 70
Meeting the Challenge 73
Memories Through Music 74
Mothers 76
Need of Direction 78
Neighbors 79
Nothing Happens 80
On The Inside 82
On The Spot Training 84
Our Place in the World 86
Overcoming 87
Overflow 89
Passing Moments 90
Power of the Spirit 92
Preparation 94
Ruling Power of Life 96
Seasons 98
Sin 99
Split Second Decision 101

Key Thoughts to Live By

by
Reed L. Hart

Published by:
HAWKES PUBLISHING, INC.
3775 South 500 West
Salt Lake City, Utah 84115
Tel. (801) 262-5555

ISBN 0-89036-133-9

Still They Accomplished.. 102
Surprise Finish 104
Symbol of Courage... 106
Teacher of Teachers... 108
That Inner Drive.. 109
The American Promise.. 111
The Beginning.. 112
The Best Years 113
The Cow Was Sold.. 115
The Coyote and The Hare... 116
The Enterprise of Living 118
The Gateway.. 120
The Greater Life 121
The Moon... 123
The Next Generation.. 124
The Seed of Life and Death...................................... 126
The Sun... 127
The Tempest Within 129
The Test... 130
They Did It... 131
To Become a Child.. 133
"To Thine Ownself Be True"..................................... 134
Too Much 136
Turning Point.. 137
Values... 139
We Are Indebted 141
Which Road 142

THE OVERVIEW

AS the world turns and the morning breaks, that untouchable future awakens to its glory; stepping into the realm of the present...and from out of eternity is born the challenge of a new day. This time flow of new beginnings belong to you and me; it's special for the best of life is projected for the living present.

WITH fragile beginnings and acceptance of things unreal, we emerge as moving targets of indirection, yet the potential of our becoming relates to the highest order of living for the season is today and now is the time for adding new wood to the soul. The night of darkness nears in which no labor is performed.

THE richness we give to life is an extension of ourselves in which blessings of return, predicated on the law of obedience are perpetual and never-ending. Our performance here is scheduled for a special reading as we pass in judgment. It will be a day of anticipation and tense moments for the season will have passed to negotiate for a more delightful settlement with the Lord.

THIS life is not a dress rehearsal on the stage of passing time...it's the real thing; the main event passing in review. The fringe benefit for having endured to the end in righteousness will be a state of celestial living; a quality glory unlimited.

NOT knowing from whence we came and why we are here is unreal, but forgetting in whose image and likeness we are created is regrettable and tragic.

AN ERA IN TIME

It was a cold day in December 1905 that my spirit took on the flesh and I became a living soul. It was on Friday and since that day, during my span of 20th century living, many things previously unheard of have come to light and burst forth in the field of advanced science and technology. A network of amazing events have developed.

With the help of a battery of experts, twelve courageous men have left their footprints on the moon. Another group of skilled technicians have split the elusive atom. It's estimated that over 90% of the scientists that have lived during the past century are now living, yet the measure of credibility isn't what has happened but what we have let happen to us.

Things transpiring during the past 100 years remains unequaled from that which has happened in any period of time since Adam; with of course a few exceptions, mainly Noah, the builder of the Ark, riding out the flood and keeping the family of man alive and intact. And there was Moses who led four hundred thousand Israelites across a sea that was too wide to swim and too deep to wade; and Jesus, the light of the world, who being born of Virgin Mary, grew to maturity and bore record of his Father and atoned for the sins of all men...taking his rightful place as a member of the Godhead. And we can't overlook the year 1820 when the heavens were opened and God the Father and his Son Jesus appeared to a young lad, Joseph Smith, and the fullness of times, the greatest of all dispensation, had its beginning.

All that we hope for and have today we owe to those who have gone before. Each of us have a different set of talents and desires that must be set free if we are to measure up to the level of responsibility. Only then do we justify the right and purpose of becoming a part of earth life.

All facets of existence on planet earth continues full speed towards an undetermined course of events, yet as we walk among the beauties of nature there comes the feeling and solemn assurance of walking hand in hand with the builders of the universe. . .a unique work of glory that's never been improved upon; rotating true to character in feeding and sustaining all life.

Just as the rays from the October sun ripen grapes in my backyard, the season of time matures the soul, and from a pool of stagnant and muddy water, the water-lily in its beauty bursts forth so pure and fair. . .nature speaks; we are the translators.

Joy comes to the heart only as useful transformation of things good come into our lives. It is then we cease to mark time and set out to live and become.

"A gentle rain makes the grass a shade greener," and as we seek out the gift and deeper meaning of life, the soul takes on a brighter glow that generates an influx of generous deeds and thoughts untainted.

APPLICATION OF RESPONSIBILITY

Medical Doctors receive training and the scientific know-how to exterminate tuberculosis, but the disease is active. Architects have the technical knowledge and ingenuity to erect homes and buildings to eliminate the slums, but they continue to exist, and there are basic skill in the field of agriculture for world wide food production, but millions starve.

It isn't having knowledge, it's the application of what is done within the frame-work of skills and learning that sets the pace and measures progress.

A noted writer has written: "I've spent my days stringing and unstringing my instrument while the song I came here to sing remains unsung," reminding each that the element of time is not only our friend but also a contender for unspent days. When failing to use time with percision application of responsibility, we often get in front of our own story; losing the way of excellence outlined for joy in living. The song we came here to sing is the melody of triumph and success. . .it's music set to life, designed for building up and intensifying the soul.

Jesus accomplished that which he set out to do, writing his own finish. . .leaving no unfinished business. He went the full distance atoning for the misbehavior of man, and that event was the moment in time when the greatest discovery in the history of man was made by women. The Mary's were the first to learn that the "Tomb was Empty," and it was during the Savior's ministry that the value of common things took on new dimensions. . . the lowly sparrow at no time fell unnoticed, and Solomon in all his glory received honorable mention, second only to the splendor and beauty of the lilies in the field, while a small seed became a sermon and the lost sheep a lost soul.

Christian behavior, through the light of Christ brings the family of man closer together, in which the gift of the Holy Spirit teaches uplifting values we cannot teach one another. There is need to condition ourselves to the wave length of knowledge and understanding if we hope to get through "customs" for a place of glory with our Father.

Scientific law deals with how the world works, not the reason why, yet we are delighted that it has worked for you and me. . .our spirits made a special trip to mother earth to receive their bodies; identifing us as the launching platform for reaching and fulfilling destiny.

The pass word for entrance into the kingdom of celestial living is total commitment to the Lord in sustaining the plan of life and salvation. . .it's the shortest distance to eternal rewards.

ART OF GROWING

The Japanese have learned the art of growing dwarfed trees by cutting the "tap root." This root is the main underground artery so basic in holding the plant in position while drawing water and nourishment from the soil. Once this dominate root is cut, the tree never develops to full maturity. From that point it depends solely on the less vigorous roots that penetrate the soil near the ground surface. The tree lives, but fails to grow.

So it is with life in attempting to build a purposeful state of existence from the wavering surface roots of society. When the ways of the world choke out and narrow the flow of spiritual nourishment, we are reduced in stature to a "Tom Thumb" size. The soul dwindles and dies for lack of wholesome nutrition.

The ingredients for sustaining growth must reach deeper than the shadows and reflections set up by the whims of men. If there is to be an enrichment of thought and inspiration to feed the whole person, roots of deep understanding must penetrate the soul.

Spiritual growth is the expansion of those inner feelings within the heart that brings joy and depth to living.

When operating with a radiant spirit, within the bounds that is honest and decent, we become encircled with promised tomorrows.

The most delightful experience of life is doing things that add beauty to each living day; things carrying us into a state of usefulness; a condition that supersedes and overshadows all other ways. R. J. Shores said, "Our hope of eternal life grows out of our love for life upon this earth which we have tried and found good."

As we penetrate the rich soil of our spiritual holdings, a new era of life is marked. We find ourselves on the higher plateau of living where joy abounds with a state of peacefulness and stability; "like the deep part of the ocean that is undisturbed by the elements that ruffle the surface."

AT THE LIVING EDGE

A large tank went rolling full speed down a country road when it came to a sudden stop. Sufficient fuel was in the tank, and there was no mechanical trouble; nothing standing in its way. What went wrong?

The officer in charge stated in dispair: "We've come to the edge of the map."

Man has ways of designing maps and blueprints to which he comes to the edge in utter confusion. To follow outlined plans for a happy life isn't difficult. . .only unusual. Today we live in a world of much unfinished thinking on the subject of the finer and more positive things relating to the richness of spiritual blessings. There is no relationship in having knowledge of high purpose living, and the way we behave. Having knowledge of things uplifting makes us more accountable for its misuse. Satan in his power of demolition, ignores the truth and his work of deception becomes an investment in stocks and bonds of perdition.

To recognize truth is one thing of importance, but to understand and live the force of its mission, as written on the divine map of eternal progression, is the highest order of excellence. The value of doing things good are on deposit and remain for keeps; they belong and become a part of that which never loses its rate of exchange.

Truth is the substance giving power of thought. . .a vitality necessary for creative thinking; bringing a flow of penetration for unlocking doors to high adventure. We live to improve, and steadfastness of purpose is the vehicle upon which all truth must ride.

Where is the cutting edge of life and a map pointing out the beginning points of intelligence? We are not the first of anything except the original of ourselves. Blood circulated before it was discovered by Harvey, and Americans were here before Columbus ran into the obstacle, America, and every woman was a child with a past before the role of mother, and babies, as predetermined on the map of eternity, make such a unique and happy way to start a civilization.

Life is still under investigation; it's elusive, yet so reachable that sooner or later there will come a chance to pass in judgment before the Lord and if we live the laws of the kingdom, not only will we be able to see, but see it all, and we can forget with safety the things we do for others and remember with promise the things others have done for us.

We are a peculiar people; always challenged by that which is beyond our command, but if we are unfailing and persistent in seeking values that are upright and honest we'll never come to the edge of the map.

BALANCE AND PURPOSE

We maneuver here ninety million miles away from the penetrating sun that warms the earth and controls the seasons. This planet earth is a part of the great solar system, turning on its axis a thousand miles an hour with such precise timing that if the rotation varied one second in every hundred years, the perfect order of law in the universe would be upset.

The Lord has created and set in motion "Worlds without number" and we operate here as a mere grain of sand on the seashore of time, yet we are of a substance, the combination of which, make up the soul of man.

In some things it's better to be uninformed than the confusion of being misinformed. Unless we have knowledge from whence we came and why we are here, the foundation is missing upon which we build in knowing who we are.

We are the purpose and cause for whom Christ died; making us special and unique among the creations. Within the potential of our becoming is a state of glory of the highest order of living where only the best is good enough.

Each new day is eventful and alive; it's more than a time of life, it's a time of duty to reach out and challenge new frontiers in the business of making life more livable. The gift of another day comes as a framework of time, in which something useful must be done to balance the scale on the side of uplifting values.

The purpose of being here is to enhance our position to the ways of the Lord; giving of ourselves in building up his kingdom. As we move into the realm of giving service, the day unfolds a celestial touch of happiness that brings joy to the heart.

Everyone contributes to life his own special treatment making the business of our being here a one-time operation. It's a lifetime, full-time job in seeking out the weightier matters of truth designed for the good of all people.

Truth that sets man free is the measuring rod by which things are measured. The intelligent application of this quality product is the beginning point towards which the fullness of living and a state of perfection have their beginning. Having knowledge of light and truth doesn't change circumstances, it changes people. . .it doesn't change landmarks, it changes lives.

BEHIND THE SCENE

At a recent worlds fair was a grand spectacle showing hundreds of flashing lights displayed in unusual patterns. The scenes were varied and beautiful as lights sparkled back and forth before the people. It was exciting moments as one man with enthusiasm made the statement: "What a miracle."

Behind the backdrop, a man in overalls was putting on the whole show. He was dedicated and skilled in his profession which brought joy to him in the pleasure it gave to others.

Doing delightful things behind the scene, in the workshop of life, is good for the soul. Giving service enriches those who serve. To succeed within, one must succeed outside himself.

The sound of "silence is the element in which great things fashion themselves." The greatest show on earth is done quietly, without the blare of trumpets. This production moves in quietly; with beauty unfolding into a million new beginnings. It's called the "glory of spring."

Behind the backdrop scenes of living, men perform some of their most noteworthy works; doing things unseen at early morning or late hours. Those are the people with undeviating steadiness of purpose, supported by integrity of character and honesty of conscience. Their work is done quietly, never calling attention to themselves.

Our thoughts, many of which are often worse than we, become the tools in the workshop of the soul. We formulate an idea and the idea challenges the spirit into action and our potential is put to its greatest test. Only as we seek out the best of things do we touch the heartstrings of understanding in attaining possession of the greater gifts of life. Failure to enhance the soul to its promised place of glory, with a desire to become a more useful person, is to have paid too high a price for any other point of destination.

We are the servants, not the creators of life and must give our best to be received of the Lord. The highest quality in the use of time, are the moments dedicated to the greater part of ourselves in doing the job expected of us to do. The quality of spiritual output determines the warmth and intense joy we bring to the lives of others. We live only once and if we do our job well, once is enough.

BLIND MOMENTS

Ulysses S. Grant was riding on a train with a few of his soldiers when at one of the stops a little old lady entered the car. She was left standing as the train moved on. There were no available seats. Mr. Grant noted the situation, stood and gave his seat to the lady for which she most graciously thanked him as she sat down.

Immediately several of his men stood and offered their seat to Mr. Grant, but he refused saying: "If your seat was not available to this lady in her need, it isn't available to me."

Courtesy stands high on the list that reveals the concerns of a gracious person. Mr. Grant, true to his inner feelings, stepped into the environment of the "second mile" and displayed elegance of manners and respect in the presence of his men. While they were reading by the lamp of their own light, they became blinded to the gift of the passing moment. Courtesy is the excellence of behavior that calls for instant accountability.

Living is made up with a variety of opportunities, many of which are lost forever in moments of indecision and delay. The one lasting frustration that unnerves the spirit is spelled out in the words, "too late."

Opportunities are never placed on a "hold pattern" to be seized at a later time. Passing gifts of the hour are on the move. Opportunities are continuous; always in tempo with the events of fleeting time into a world of the unknown.

Too often in foolish moves we leave our "change" on the counter, so to speak, and experience the sting of losing something good and fine within. The scars of misbehavior and lost opportunity leave their mark to torment and obscure the view of things that matter most. When we let the world become "too much" of us, it blocks out the best. . .it is then we become strangers to the higher value of exchange.

Within our reach is a positive element with deep meaning. This special agent unlocks doors, opens the heart and enhances the day. With generating power of goodwill, it replaces prejudices with pleasure and high hopes. This spiritual commodity inspires the love of everyone, giving unique service as gifts to life. No one condemns it, all look up and admire the quality of its character. Operating in high and low places, it is needed every passing hour of the day. In its high reaching mission, it refines the spirit and perpetuates the soul to a position of dignity and polish. The elegance of this life sustaining service is called "courtesy."

"A gracious person sees more in what he sees in others, not less, and because he sees more, he willingly sees less."

CONSIDER THE END

The will of God was fulfilled through the mission of His Son Jesus whose death was timely and acceptable of his Father. The Savior fulfilled the outlined plan of life for the redemption of all men.

The work of Judas, who betrayed the Savior, was approved of the Devil, the master planner of all evil and who delights when another chapter of atrocious acts are added to his book of perdition and lost souls.

The course of human history is rough and smooth. The divine plans of the Lord are not changed to satisfy the impatience and desires of men.

There was a man who had lost his way, leaving a note behind saying: "I leave society a bad example. I leave to my friends a memory of a misspent life. And, to my father and mother I leave all the sorrow they can bear in their old age. I leave my wife a broken heart. To my children, I leave the name of a drunkard and a suicide. I leave to God a lost soul who has insulted his memory." Each of us must give an account. There is nothing so final as a life having been lived.

There are two subject matters relating to the destination of man that must be considered. The first and foremost is knowing who we are, and secondly with integrity of purpose to consider the end. To understand either takes a lifetime of dedicated work and study. Having knowledge from whence we came, the purpose of the trip, and an awareness there's no end to new beginnings, places us on the open road to greater discoveries. To consider the end is knowing there's a cut-off point in mortality and the life of the spirit never dies.

In this period of "test-living" there are two important subjects which all men should be interested in—the gift of life and the purpose of death. Jesus was concerned about both, for he said: "I am the resurrection and the life; he that believeth in me, though he were dead, yet shall he live."

An earthquake may bury us, a fire consume, and water drown us, but no force can stay the redeeming power of God. This worthwhile come with the price of effort. Many treasures gathered in passing this way are not "home free," but are subject to the test of time. To almost save your soul is complete failure. One can't explode the atomic bomb a little. The roots of a tree will not penetrate dry soil regardless of how much moisture lies near the surface. Sometimes we live within inches of truth and light of knowledge, yet dwell in darkness.

We can't reshape things we do not control; at best, however, we can reshape ourselves to the ways of the Lord in putting together a life that is acceptable and worthy of honorable mention for a place in His kingdom.

CREATIVE POWER WITHIN

The key function of life is challenging the human spirit to better itself in bringing out the best within. There is little justification for the passing of this day unless from it we expand spiritual boundaries with understanding hearts in moving upward to a more satisfying level of performance.

The true character of man isn't developed in storms nor the front line of conflicts, it is merely revealed and brought to public notice. It's from the trial and adventures of living that advance and reinforces the true measure of man.

Few, if any, know the limits of their natural abilities for so little of the capacities within have been put to use. This unused realm of potential is wasted life until generated into action. "It is the lack of purpose, not the shortage of talent, that causes men to fail."

Helen Keller lived in a world without color and without sound, yet she created light, sound and order within herself that the outer world could not penetrate. Real discoveries are not reached in seeking new landscapes, but in penetrating the hidden opportunities within the landscape that is presently occupied.

Everyone has a spark of creative power on standby waiting for the right person to cross his or her path and bring it to action. It's the positive talents we put into motion that become the moving force of life.

We must be true to ourselves, to the gift of expression, for there are those who trust and depend on us. Unless we stay on course, upholding the purpose and dignity of our responsibility, we become distorted to the image in whose likeness we are created.

In accepting the best of things spiritual, and giving ourselves to others, we travel first class on the open road of life. In our day to day living we are sometimes criticized for things we do, and in other things receive little praise, but when we bring useful changes into the life of others, we receive the praise of all men.

Knowledge that enhances the soul is without bounds . . .working overtime. Every age extends it, every good book enlarges upon it, and every alert mind adds the intelligence of moral soundness to it.

COURTSHIP

The one thing we remember best about the writings of Jacob in the Old Testament is that he was the father of the twelve tribes of Israel.

Jacob with his wives and family of sons encountered many problems along the way, just as we today have similar problems. Sooner or later life gives everyone their portion of trouble; no one has the know-how to escape.

Jacob had marriage difficulties. He worked seven years for the right to marry Rachel, the daughter of Laban, but he was paid with her sister Leah. In that era of time it was customary to marry off the oldest daughter first.

When the heavy veil was removed from the face of the bride, Rachel was missing and there stood Leah. This was indeed a discouraging blow to deal a man of forty years. However, Laban, the father-in-law, was very generous. He made another bargain with Jacob, saying, "take Rachel" now and work seven more years. That's the way it happened. Having proven his credibility and trust, he labored again for seven years on the installment plan and came into full possession of his first choice, the second daughter, Rachel. Jacob was then forty-seven years of age, and his life was just beginning. He never permitted seven additional years of soul testing change his course.

The one mark of greatness was his exhibition of patience during the extended years of his courtship.

There was Jonah, the run-away prophet, who refused to die easy, and there was John the Baptist, the forerunner to the dispensation of Jesus, who prepared the way of his coming. And there was Saul of Tarsus who hunted down the Christians, but later with a change of heart "spoke with a new tongue." Unlike these, Jacob stayed at home where he tilled the soil, took care of the flocks and reared his children.

There are many good quarter horses, but those of this variety and class who can keep up a fast pace for a mile are few indeed. Jacob proved himself with stability and enduring qualities; finishing the course over the greater distance in full command of his calling.

Nothing fulfills and satisfies like involvement in attaining goals one sets out to reach. Strength and quality determination carried Jacob forward in setting up the house of Israel. He considered the end from the beginning and made things happen.

The most lasting monuments we leave posterity are not the markers built of marble or stone, but in the excellence of living, doing ordinary things well and passing them along for the greater gifts.

CYCLE OF YEARS

As the cycle of years roll on, few people realized that the abundant life is essentially the life of the spirit. Those born again of the spirit are receipients of ". . .tidings of great joy;" for joy is the gift of the spirit, and "happiness is the object and design of our existence."

Seeking less of things that matter most has been the trademark of men from the beginning, yet when this life ends, a most challenging part of the journey, to enhance the soul, has just begun.

Understanding and applying laws that spotlights the soul is a function and degree of the highest intelligence. Having a knowledge that God is our Father is better than having the know-how of splitting the atom; and greater riches come through having a testimony that Jesus, the Son of God, atoned for the sins of man, than reaching planets in outer space.

Opportunities of the present are the points of beginning for expanding old boundaries into new fields of challenge. What we are now can never measure up to what we may become through living the perfect order in helping others along the way. The method used to calibrate the quality of our performance is assessed by the application of time...how it was used to enhance the soul.

It was Peter who remembered, as the cock crowed at an early hour, that he in his moments of weakness had denied knowing the Savior three times. His lips momentarily overruled the heart and he became a dejected soul. Peter had considered his denials as the easy way out, but learned with sorrow that an untruth is hard to bear and only the light of truth is the standard by which all things are measured.

It isn't necessary for the cock to crow, as with Peter, to remind us wherein we have failed the Lord. The voice of the spirit within conveys the message; but we must listen ...it never shouts. In moments of prayer and meditation, the message will find its way to the heart.

DAVID AND KING SAUL

The most deép-seated and moving battle between two biblical personalities for the Kingship was the running encounter between David and King Saul.

David, in his desire for leadership, refused to become king by assination, by killing the Lord's anointed. Therefore, David's battle became one of respect, of escape and defense. At an early age David had gained a keen perception of the greater values of things lasting. He was master of his emotions.

During their hit and run tactics, David contained the wisdom to restrain the many chances to take the life of his king, while Saul in his intermittent rages sought out the life of his rival.

Saul lived from day to day on a suspended sentence, while David in his waiting tactics played for higher stakes.

It was the battle of the century; a conflict between love and hate, between loyalty and respect, and a conniving spirit that was bound up with an intense desire to eliminate and destroy.

Showing respect for authorized leaders is the "seal of obedience" that refines the spirit to a place of usefulness in the society of men. Obedience is fundamental to the laws that govern both heaven and earth in keeping nations and people operating with dignity and with vigor of purpose on a friendly level.

A firmness of loyalty to those holding positions of trust must be sustained in any land, and mainly in the hearts of people if peace is to fly its banner. Only through having respect for recognized leaders will there come a greater spiritual output for the blessings of men.

We may disagree with the acts of those in authority, but in this free land, we must not disagree in giving them the full right to exercise responsibility of direction in their constituted power to act.

The scale of our accountability must be balanced against that which is expected of us, and that which is done.

King Saul became a prisoner of himself. He ruled a nation but failed to solve problems at his own door step.

Little thought is needed to destroy, but much thought is necessary to be right. Every wrong decision is the beginning point on the downside of living.

Some things we do in seeking out the best in life is failure, while many things we succeed in doing is tragedy. It isn't necessary to "eat a whole sheep to know what mutton tastes like" nor participate in sin to know the waste of evil.

We go onward and up, or gravitate into obscurity.

DECEPTION

As a growing boy I learned the secret of trapping muskrats in the swamps near Bear River. There are several ways of catching this fur-bearing animal, one of which is the dryland method. It's successful by setting a trap near the water's edge with a stick extended about fifteen inches high having a piece of apple placed at the top.

There is usually one animal that steps into the trap during the process of reaching for the bait. When the jaws snap, by nature the muskrat attempts an escape by diving into the water. The weight of the trap holds it under and it becomes the victim of deception and a cunning scheme set up by conniving man.

In life we carelessly set our own trap in which we become the first victim being caught in the web of circumstances of our own making; drowning in the flood of dispair.

As we move through the various channels of living, most things learned are merely branches to the tree of knowledge and understanding, not the tree itself.

Having the light of Christ is the birthright of every living person, and if this glow of understanding goes out, man soon adapts himself to a condition of darkness and a state of enslaved living. Until this light is rekindled, the glow of intelligence remains dim and the footprints of man are seen in the shadows.

In premortal life, the Devil with his self imposed power, generated an all-out war among the spirit children of God. Today on earth with his agents, this author of destruction continues the same war. . .a contest of nation fighting against nation, truth against error, and light against darkness. Condemning man is the role of Lucifer who performs so successful in his kingdom of desolation and perdition. His field of operations however, are off-limits to those of integrity and moral soundness.

The most difficult lessons learned here among the many choices are the things that must be done first to enhance one's position of trust for a place in the realm of celestial living.

The lack of knowledge and understanding of the divine plan of life and salvation, narrows the field of choice and brings frustration and early defeat to the soul, while the application of things pertaining to intelligent life, relates to perpetual growth. . .unlocking the door to the highest order of happiness.

Blessings never come from broken laws of deceptions and commandments unlived.

ELEMENT OF TIME

The Giant Goliath roared with laughter when he was challenged by a young lad named David. It was only a matter of one stone and two minutes later that Goliath lay dead and a nation saved. It was the shortest battle on record. It took Moses forty years in the wilderness to save the Hebrews.

The affairs of history never just happen—they are brought about, and during the process no one holds the power to withstand the march of events. In the matter of success or failure, life or death, the element of time is unyielding and rigid. It never erases history; but through change, buries it.

People are not weak by choice. Many reach "hard bottom" seeking after a loaf of bread when a slice is sufficient. Success is basic to our wants and comes from doing that which is necessary in fulfilling a need.

Each morning we line up at the same starting point at which time we exhibit our better selves. At night we add up the score. We are usually strong in the early hours, weak in the afternoon, and quite unnerved and powerless at night. Peter was strong at the break of day. His weakness flared up at the evening hour, and it took the crow of the cock to remind him that he had denied the Savior three times. It was nighttime when Judas betrayed Jesus with a kiss, but it's the shining light of truth that is fatal to the work of the Devil, whose most destructive manipulations are done in the shadows. We learn many important lessons from sad experiences, all because Satan has mastered the art of taking away and denaturing the best of the qualities in us.

David's battle with Goliath was a precision performance in split second timing, while the life and struggle of Moses is measured on the calendar of years, yet both men did their jobs within the limits of time.

From birth unto death is a "time interval;" a time frame, not a time movement. The hands on a clock is a movement of time. The clock is an object in space that measures the day, just as the rotating earth with the stability of the sun is the great universal time clock measuring the movements of the seasons and the civilized state of man.

Within the framework of passing moments we are expected to build a life. Many things we do seem unreal for we fail in taking time to do a thing right the first time, yet we have time to do it over. It's part of the learning process. It takes many grains of sand to build mountains as moments soon become years, but it's the trifles of indifference and misjudgment that consumes a life. Every thought has a destination—good or bad.

The best way to choke out noxious weeds is to cultivate the flowers.

ERA OF ABUNDANCE

We live in an age of full measure. From the beginning of the 19th century we have produced and manufactered a pyramid of material goods for both happiness and sorrow. Skills have been developed to shorten and prolong life. Many scientific advancements have evolved with more comforts and better ways of living and dying. However, with all the improved things of today over generations past, we have yet to discover a more inviting and lofty place to go, to attain, to reach for, than the place called "home." It continues to be the most satisfying and delightful place on this planet earth for the family of man. A home with its love and sharing, is a reflection of things good that are basic for happiness and joy in the kingdom of our Father...a place designed for celestial living. There is no higher point of destination with greater promise to challenge the soul.

In this life there are no substitute for a kind word, the worth of a smile, friends, a loving home and family. This combination is the hub of civilized life. Spiritual growth relates to the higher plateau of living where with dignity the family may be enthroned to a state of exaltation.

In this pleasure-seeking world of sensation to sensation, the ten commandments, through all their abuse and testing, remains self-contained and the most accurate measure of calculating the distance between the behavior of man and the potential of his becoming. From the beginning a renewal of the spirit and the right of choice, have been subject to the law of obedience, both here and in premortal living. This principle and "agency of choice" was dated before matter was organized, the world set in motion, and man placed here.

Among the network of struggles in this computer age, there are no short cuts yet developed to advance the time schedule of the Lord. His second coming is set by revelation to come in its own appointed hour. There is work to be done for the keys of the resurrection have not yet been given to man.

There can be no thunder clap before the lightning comes, nor is there a short cut in the distance of the hundred-yard dash; and no secret back door entrance to the Kingdom of the Lord. There's one entrance only, the door of which is constructed to open only when the celestial touch of the soul unlocks it from the inside.

EVENT IN HISTORY

In the year 1776 there appeared a news item in a leading newspaper that read: "Rev. Wittenspoon took part in the congressional deliberation last week in which he stated that this country is not only ripe for independence but in danger of becoming rotten for the lack of independence."

Many patriots of that day shared the vision of the Reverend Wittenspoon and consequently today July 4th of each year is celebrated as the birthday of a great nation.

Seven years following this declaration of the people, the final peace articles of war were signed on September 3, 1783. The first British soldiers, after eight years of war in America, sailed out of the New York Harbor November 23, 1784, and in the later part of 1787 the constitution was set up by inspired leaders.

The Bill of Rights was written and accepted by the people in 1789; however, this document added nothing to the Constitution. It merely reserved certain rights and conditions in the constitution specifically for the people themselves.

And so America had its beginning as a nation with freedom to govern itself. Since that momentous day, this government has gone through four great crisis: The year it was born; when it was divided; when it became of age; and now in maturity, it is being put to its greater test. It has become a disease with some nations to covet that which is good and attractive of which is America. Because we are the treasure house of the earth, this nation is marked for "plunder" by other powers.

Citizens of America must continue to be a society of responsible people. It's a great nation because leaders have conditioned themselves to spiritual values. It is not a country of merchandise alone; it commands a balance of power. Family life is the safety-valve. No country long endures after the home disintegrates, for it is there a nation suffers its first defeat.

The constitution of this land has been constant and deep-rooted. It has been shaken, but it stands firm and alert. Those who dwell here love this land. The wealth and quality in this place of choice is bound up in the character and integrity of the people.

Freedom is the first word disappearing from the vocabulary of dictators, who little realize that the stability and real strength of a nation is built on spiritual foundations. The compelling force of freedom within the heart of man is the most effective weapon of defense.

The Lord, in setting up his earthly kingdom some 1900 years ago, said: "Let not my house be a house of merchandise." Merchandise misused is the trouble spot of the earth and man becomes the first casualty. For the soul to reach maturity and become a finished product is hard to come by. It has happened only once. It was Jesus the

Carpenter, the Son of Mary, the Lord and Savior, the Redeemer of all men.

"EXCEPT A MAN IS BORN..."

Perhaps the office hours Jesus kept were irregular for it was Nichodemus, the ruler of the Jews, who may have been too busy making money in the daytime, sought out the Savior at night. He didn't come to discuss the law of the fast, nor the secret of turning water into wine, nor the wage and hour law. He came to inquire how he, Nichodemus, could conveniently get himself into the Kingdom of God.

He received a clear and simple answer: "Except a man is born of water and of the spirit he cannot enter into the Kingdom of God."

Jesus exalted the spirit of man over the body, yet there were those who looked upon him with impure hearts and reported they saw in him a "winebibber." When Jesus prayed to God his Father, they called him a blasphemer and as he paid "truth" it's highest tribute that "it shall make you free" he was called the servant of the Devil, claiming he deceived the people.

Only as we are taught by the spirit can we understand "things as they are and as they really will be." The knowledge and understanding gained through teachings of the life and mission of Jesus reaches beyond all other forms of learning. During His reign among men were followers who looked to Him, the carpenter's son, as a political potential, qualified to liberate the people and unshackle them from the grip of Roman power. Many looked to Him as this liberator and missed seeing Him as the Son of God, the Redeemer of the world.

The Devil is a master of deception. He never presents things as they are. Not everything we learn here will be useful in the next state of living; in fact some things learned could spiritually destroy us. Paul says: We are "ever learning and never able to come to the knowledge of the truth." Through deceptive methods we are taken in by ourselves, acting against our own best interest, locking ourselves out. We trade the "real-thing" for the trade-offs, letting fleeting pleasures of the "now of life" swallow us up.

The world is full of inequalities rising out of the stupidities of man sprinkled with an array of doubts and suspended judgment through lack of light and knowledge.

It's unreal to accept the knowledge that Jesus is the Christ without accepting facts about the realness of the Devil. Only when we pass the "exaltation test" and receive a passing mark will there be a place for us in the upper classroom of celestial learning.

The test that must not fail is the final examination of total commitment in serving the Lord. Anything short of having gained this awareness dissolves itself and there comes a point when earthly glory and praises of men are no longer heard. . .the bubble bursts and the cheering stops. Today is the hour to lift our sights. . .to broaden our vision. . .turn the corner and move in a direction that brings self-conquest to the soul.

FREE SPIRIT

The most satisfying act for enhancing the joy of living is not the power to rule over men, but having the gift of direction to serve among men. Helping those in need is a most generous way to intensify the spirit. It's a personal service that carries within the heart a bond of devotion; an unbroken chain of love that has no bounds. When we step into the second mile of giving service we share in the management of our Father's business. It's an exercise that fills the "Cup that Runneth Over," spilling into eternity.

The feel of being wanted and accepted; to be used up in bringing progressive change into the lives of others, is a joy that only the heart can measure.

Freedom of the spirit is the key for a happy and fulfilling life.

It was Nadya Stalin, the wife of the Dictator, Joseph Stalin of Russia, who told her daughter, at a young age, to never "touch alcohol; never drink wine." Mrs. Stalin had seen her son die an alcoholic. She knew the curse of liquor.

It was in the month of October that Stalin and other leaders had met to celebrate the 15th anniversary of the Russian revolution. The group were drinking and as Stalen raised his glass, he glanced to the side and saw his wife Nadya. He shouted! "Hey you, have a drink." She screamed back; "Don't you dare, hey me!" and in front of everyone she got up and ran from the table. The next morning they found in her hand a pistol as she lay in a pool of blood. She had shot herself; withdrawing from life rather than give up her ideals. All the wife of Stalin wanted was his respect. Her desires were to be recognized as a person; one of dignity and not classified as an object of ridicule. Being a lady of principle, with freedom of spirit, she refused to be a part of the environment in which she found herself.

People with integrity of purpose are self-contained, deep-rooted and unfailing in reaching for the greater values.

There is only one decisive failure and that's the person who isn't true to the best he knows. Living a good example is the pure language of thought.

We are the engineers of what we become. If we leave the weeds alone they soon choke out the flowers. There is a choice. We can hold to the higher ideals and grow or let malnutrition of thought rule the day and deplete the soul.

The abundant life is essentially the life of the spirit, bringing joy to the heart with peace of mind.

We are daily confronted with decision making problems as Nadya Stalin. A disciplined life is in outline in bringing to the surface the higher riches. In meeting today's challenge there is need to take a stand where we are, lest we become wanders on the dusty road of confusion.

FINAL NOTICE

We cast our lot with many enterprising ventures. Why not take a chance doing business with the Lord? Peter did. He gave up fishing; left his boats and nets and took a chance on dry land. Things turned out well. He faltered occasionally, but staying on course he delivered the message and cast the Gospel net on the otherside of the boat. . .launching deep into the hearts of men. Things began to happen. A new movement evolved. People walked the earth more stately. Hearts were touched and spiritual settings came anew. Life took on a restored outlook as the followers of Jesus caught the meaning in the words: "Know the truth and the truth shall make you free."

In his message of hope, Jesus exalted the spirit over the body, yet his enemies insisted that he modify his program to suit their demands or be eliminated, but the Lord at no time disguises truth to appease contentions among men. Again we have been given the "final notice" that no man can be saved in ignorance of the saving principles of the gospel. His doctrine is the key to life everlasting that can't wait to be discovered. . .it must be declared.

We have a right to our own opinions regarding politics, taxes and the price of wheat, but when we discuss things pertaining to the kingdom of God we must be sure about destiny and capture the message: "Except a man is born of water and of the spirit, he cannot enter the kingdom of God." Exaltation is everybodies business, for both living and dead and the opportunity will present itself to the souls of all men for acceptance or rejection to the plan of salvation.

The fullness of God's state of glory relates to those who honor his name in obedience and return in righteousness to dwell with him forever. Man has been well advised on things he must do to identify himself with things positive and uplifting, for the future reveals the greater reward to those who prepare for its coming, while the life of the present brings to notice the challenge, that no one has the gift and ability to succeed alone; he must take with him, someone else.

Living among us are those having more faith, in the wrong things, than they know what to do with, which is equal in substance as those going full speed ahead in the wrong direction.

It's when we overlook seeing the potential power and freedom of things beautiful in others that we fail to appreciate and breath deeply of life about us.

FLORENCE NIGHTINGALE

Florence Nightingale wrote in her diary, "On my 31st birthday I see nothing desirable but death." She in her despondent moments was having more trouble with herself than any other person, but she awakened to realities, and a new and purposeful life unfolded.

Everyone is equal in opportunities to grow into something positive and acceptable. It's the application of the gifts within that reveals the real person.

To become a shining light that others admire, it is paramont that we know who we are, our identity, and in whose spiritual likeness we are in design to become. To have integrity of purpose in expanding the soul to greater heights is to crack the shell of complacency and surrender to the voice of understanding.

Florence Nightingale came into her own and accepted what she had to do, giving an account and becoming true to the deep within drive. She recognized many things more desirable than death and accepted the challenge to live.

There is a continuous supply of things that freely camouflage the view for success in living. The greatest restraint seems to be that ever-flowing supply of confusion tainted with organized deception. We too often fail to see the kernal of truth, the golden key that opens the door to many riches. Florence found the treasures that gave her an "overflow" of inner satisfaction, bringing joy to the heart.

A demanding rule to follow in life was given by a mother to her complaining child when she said, "Look here son, I gave you life, now get busy and do something with it."

As we live the answers to the difficult questions of the day, we confirm the validity and purpose of life. We move ahead only as we filter from the mind thoughts and ideas that are not related to the splendor of things spiritual.

We have a right to life, but we have no claim in taking more from it than we earn. . .more than we return. We have been given the right to live, but we have no business neglecting our duty of responsibility at the risk of hurting and bringing hardship to others.

"A low place in the field after a storm drinks its own rain and the rain of its neighbors." We must rise to our potential to live and become.

FOR WHOM DO WE WORK?

Eugene Field, a noted columnist, sent a note to the editor of a daily paper saying: "There will be no news column from me tomorrow; life is too hard, I'm giving up."

The Editor replied, "I have an employee working in the basement who has a wife and three children with scarlet fever. He's in debt and things are not going well. He isn't giving up."

The next day's news column from Mr. Field arrived at the Editor's desk on time.

From the piccolo to the bass drum and loud cymbal, everyone must play their part in the orchestra of life's symphony. A part missing brings confusion to the players and disappointment to the Great Conductor.

We never become better without making someone else better. We may not sing the same harmony part together, but if there is to be music, we must be in the same key. Unless bees work in harmony together, there is no honey.

While living in this complex society, we establish a dependence on one another, yet a most common mistake among men is believing they are working for someone else. First and foremost, man works for himself for he is responsible to himself and must give an accounting. When the goodness and overflow of ones best efforts are shared with others, that is the moment he has done a most delightful and useful service for himself.

The most effective work we do isn't truly our own until it is given in part to help others along the way. Elbert Hubbard said: "An uplifting thought is not our own until we have passed it to another."

The morning Eugene Field changed his mind and sent his daily news article to the Editor was his most productive work and most satisfying hour. Life took on new meaning. He became the recipient of an untroubled mind with an understanding heart. Things suddenly became beautiful and good to him.

Every talent has a responsibility to another. Most things we do for ourselves dies with us, unless it is done for the good of others. Only then does it belong.

The Lord is in the business of saving souls. When he said: "For behold this is my work and my glory to bring to pass the immortality and eternal life of man," he was referring to a program designed for the salvation of man in bringing added glory to His Kingdom. He further stated: ". . .and worlds without number have I created . . .and I created them for mine own purpose. . .for they are mine." In His creative work the glory of all things are centered with Him, bringing an abundant overflow of blessings to the souls of all mankind.

While reaching out for a happy life, we have learned various ways of trading wisdom for information; tradition for fashion and lasting joy for passing pleasure. The gifts outlined for purposeful living were designed especially for you and me and as we become happy, it brings hopes for others to be happy. Even in our unperfected bodies, designed as the caretakers of the spirit, we are God's greatest miracle; his highest creation. This is our day to identify ourself with the best.

FRIENDS

Friendship begins within the heart as an expression of the soul. With cultivation it becomes a moving force of devotion and fellowship evolving into a state of happiness.

Sometime ago I met an old friend whom I hadn't seen for many years. We were both surprised in seeing how unkind the years had been as it showed up in the character lines of our faces. During conversation, I knew his spirit had mellowed and his life, having been so heavy laden with worldly deceptions, had favored him.

During our renewal of friendship he mentioned how foolish it was of him, during his younger days, to have convicted within his heart on circumstantial evidence, many of his passing acquaintances who are today among his choice friends. He said, "In my snap judgment I failed to see the real person deep within, and through the years I have carried memories of regret, but how greatful I am today for friends, for the change that has come to me through them."

Misusing the gift of friends is the downfall of man in attempts to become a responsible person. Written at the core of human life is the law of love and friendship of kindness and stability of understanding.

One person declared: "I set out to find a friend, but couldn't find one. I set out to be a friend, and friends were everywhere."

The need of friends is inseparately connected with the life of man. Having no friends is "Paradise lost," for without friendship and devotion, life is so deadly.

Friends are those who carry an inner glow of understanding that is grown in the rich soil and warm personal feeling of love.

Perhaps the greatest waste of potential is the love that was never given and the gift of understanding never used. This life is a venture in which we come into focus with the reality of things that shapes destiny. We may not control the length of years, but we have control over that which we contribute to this day. We may not command direction of opportunity that come to others, but we can grasp our own. A good deed performed in China carries the same reward as a good deed on a crowded bus in America.

FROM OUT OF THE PAST

From the beginning, noted leaders have left their niche in history, marking off intervals of time for others to reflect and draw upon.

It is recorded that Cain, the tiller of the soil, slew his brother Abel, the keeper of the sheep. And with his, "Am I my brother's keeper" attitude, Cain apparently got away with murder except that the Lord held him in contempt and set a mark upon his head as a sign that he would not die before his permitted time.

Cain was the first casualty becoming the Devil's good news of damnation. It was the beginning of trouble in the land.

It is also written that Enoch and his people, who walked in righteousness, reached a state of perfection;

and as a reward for their "heaven and earth" performance they were permitted to by-pass the grave and be taken up in a state of glory, having earned a short-cut in time to the blessings of the Kingdom. Their love and obedience to the ways of God over-ran the bounds of mortal life.

The bible tells about a flood in which the Lord permitted every person to drown that Noah didn't convert. He preached one hundred twenty years and didn't convert anyone except his family. When the boat was finished and the rains came, those on land were looking up in despair, for they were to be lost in a waste of water.

Abraham, the father of the faithful, appeared on the biblical scene. He and his son Isaac went into the mountains on a father's and son's outing; and Abraham in his attempt to sacrifice Isaac to the Lord, failed in his efforts. A ram was provided for the fire, and the seed of Israel preserved. They came out of the mountain as they had gone up, and perhaps young Isaac pondered in his mind the question that was ask in that crucial moment, "Behold the wood and the fire, but where is the lamb?"

There is the moving story of Joseph who was sold for a slave by his brothers to an Egyptian caravan. The jealous brothers take home pay for their business transaction was twenty pieces of silver. In deceit, they returned to their father Jacob, the coat of Joseph dipped in blood.

The bible relates how Joseph rose from the bottom of the pit to become Prime Minister of Egypt. In later years Joseph's father, with his sons, "who knew him not," but who hungered for food, bowed down to him for he had corn.

There is also recorded a story about a great prophet and teacher who was "slow of speech." His name was Moses. Under his leadership came the Ten Commandments, and during the forty years of struggle in the wilderness, he prepared the children of Israel for a land of promise...their destination, yet as their leader he was no longer permitted to lead and was left behind. He died in the schoolroom of fire, the land of the "burning bush"...a bush that was never consumed. It was the second time fire was discovered by man, but Moses discovered it in its purest form.

GEORGE WASHINGTON

C. D. Ross said that no one would dare slap George Washington on the back and call him "George." Yet Mr. Washington took off his hat and bowed to an old slave who had first tipped his hat and said: "Good Mo'nin General Washington." General Lafayette who accompanied Washington asked, "why he would bow to a slave?" The answer came: "I would not permit him to be a better gentleman than I am."

Our first President of this, the "promised land" of America, refused to be less than he was. He became a leader and a gentleman making up the fullness of his leadership, the total person. He contained the conviction within, that all men are born to the right of equal treatment and that the motivating cause of equality outlined for the people is bigger than the ways of man.

Washington refused to let difficulties seal up the fate of his country. He lived with difficulties, walked with them, and in them found his strength. Overcoming problems were commanding moments of satisfaction in his life. He sought help and learned early in life that "prayer was the most powerful form of energy to be generated."

Justice Hugo Black said of George Washington, that "he wasn't the greatest intellect, the greatest speaker, or the greatest strategist. . .he was the greatest man." Leo Rosten wrote, "of those who have imagination, few have something called 'judgment'." The ability to judge saved this country because of one man, George Washington.

Most of us have been companions to trouble; there is need for adversity. Without difficulties, hidden powers would never be used. There could be things we would never experience, and most important, the feelings of love for others we could never know.

The humble and meek are not only the chosen people of the earth. . .they are the elect. Their lives inherit a spiritual setting that is concerned with all life. Their communication isn't so much in speaking with one another as in reaching others. Just as the apple drops close to the tree and a child lives close to its mother, the elect are near the Lord and become the pulsebeat and movement that is the foundation and life blood of all honest people.

The best thing about "we the people" of America, is that "we can bring about change in our society without throwing people in jail; without torturing them, bringing change through discussion and without violence."

The greatest tragedy of life is living in the ruins of our neglect.

The spirit of the Lord is the same spirit that is bound up in the law of freedom and agency of choice that operated in premortal life before man became a living soul.

Washington not only recognized the right and dignity of slaves, but in his heart honored them.

GUARANTEE

There are retail stores that guarantee some products as long as ten years. Other items carry a ninety day warranty while some goods can't be guaranteed overnight. The scale of values are varied according to the nature of the product and the stuff it's made of.

All men should be active stockholders in the business of selling a product that surpasses all others. It never depreciates, wears out or loses its market value. This sought after item is accepted among people the world over and operates beyond the reach of moth and rust. Inflation lacks power to reduce its worth. This special item is the product of truth that carries an everlasting guarantee.

Birth into this life carries no guaranty that we shall live beyond the next sunset, but with every birth comes a warranty or guarantee, written in the blood of the atoning sacrifice of the Savior that we shall live again. . .an assurance that we never meet here for the last time.

When Jesus, age twelve, stood among doctors and learned men, he was missed by Joseph and Mary; yet he wasn't lost. He had merely entered into big business at an early age; his Father's business. It was a process of learning and teaching preparatory to his climatic mission, the atoning sacrifice for the blessing of all men. To live again is a right not a choice. The choice was made in premortal life when we chose to come here and confront every conceivable thing to enrich or destroy the soul.

From our view in premortal living we saw the cycle of life, birth, death and the resurrected state of man. We beheld things of the future that would endure and count most. Only as we do things of most importance first may we safely let the lesser significant things take their chance on getting done. We must be very selective in choice for doing things wrong never fills the vacuum it creates. Within the soul each has a spark of intentness that seeks for something more satisfying than merely living in a state of existence. It isn't what we have or know about things that gives satisfaction, it's the way the heart feels and accepts things coming our way that brings joy to the soul.

Difficulties come to all of us, but the complexity of problems to some folks are no problems at all to those who understand the purpose and design for the greater life. Honest work, uplifting deeds and creativity of higher values bring joy to living, which in itself has a unique way of defrosting the chill of indifference. It's "when we light up the pathway of those in need, that we see more clearly our own."

Reaching the highest success in the realm of living relates to those who serve more people better than others.

GUIDING LIGHT

The Artic Tern is the champion long distance migrant bird of the world. From its winter to summer home is 11,000 miles, 22,000 miles round trip.

Intelligent man hasn't the slightest idea how this seasonal bird and others get the signal when to take flight, where to go, and the hour of return, but the message gets through. They must leave or die. . .having that built-in safety valve as part of their creation, the light of instinct giving direction that preserves life.

"The light of Christ is the spirit that giveth light to every man that cometh into the world. . ." and without the sunlight vegetation could not grow, and without "the breath of life" birds and other species could not exist. The divine spark that gives light and life to the world "is the law by which all things are governed."

The spirit of man has no ending, but there are restrictions to other living species of life. "Flowers that smile today die tomorrow." Everyone and things are necessary to someone else, but man with his indepth power and talents is mainly responsible to himself. His soul must be saved and accounted for. All living things relate to the gift of intelligent life to which each become a vital part.

It has been estimated that the power output of an average huricane releases as much energy, with equivalent force, to keep United States in electricity for fifty years. Light travels around our little world 7½ times a second. A diamond is a chunk of coal that made good under pressure, it's unique in the way it spits up light as no other gem does—being the hardest substance known, yet it has "come to pass." All things are a part of and basic to the governing laws of this planet earth.

This era of time makes up the stream of life in which we live and die, and there must come peace within lest our most valued treasures are submerged in the downpour of passing events.

This is our set apart day to become pioneers in successful living. Let it be said, "this day we sailed on course" and simplified our way of thinking to the voice of the soul.

HAPPINESS AT HOME

The King being stricken with a strange disease was told if he could wear the shirt of a happy person, he would be cured. He immediately sent his men in search of his happiest subject, and when they found him, he had no shirt.

Material goods relate to happiness, but having desirable things never guarantee a state of well-being. It's the application of the things uplifting that challenge the spirit to a state of happiness—It may be beautifying the home, planting and cultivating a garden, or doing other delightful things, bringing joy within. Happiness isn't a free traded item, it can't be purchased on the open market. It must be acquired. It emerges from things spiritual, from friends and family. It can't be shared until it's generated.

The noblest concept of man is the knowledge that family units will continue in glory beyond the grave.

A most vital application of thought in bringing joy to the heart is bound up in the words: "God is Love." To love our Father in Heaven is a positive force. Spreading His light of understanding along the way beautifies the spirit to the point we may "be the candle or the mirror that reflects His light" for a state of quality living.

The Lord doesn't say much in the New Testament about homes, but a great deal is said about the essential ingredients for happy home life. Things basic to peaceful living 1900 years ago are vital for happiness today. Love and respect must be companion volumes if happiness is to take its place in the family circle. Having an uncomplaining spirit of kindness and respect for others make up the home fixtures that become the foundation upon which the family builds its identity for evermore.

Speaking of man and wife, the architects of the home, John Ruskin has written: "Each has what the other has not; each completes the other; they are nothing alike; and happiness and perfection of both depends on each asking and receiving from the other what the other only can give."

From the beginning of time "goodly parents" have been the central figure of the home; a going concern making up the life-blood of mankind.

Each revolving day brings the merry-go-round of life into focus. The soul must be saved this trip around for there is no second chance to pilot another voyage, making today's assignment all important if we are to ready ourselves for an elect place in the kingdom of many mansions.

HELEN KELLER

Artists in their creativity make the canvass speak and the marble live. Medical doctors and nurses have lengthened life and conquered pain. Musicians, with their talents, have given their soul to sound, and industrialists and scientists have changed the way of life among men. Those who have worked the soil have produced well, bringing joy and balance to living.

Great accomplishments, however, are but one facet to the welfare of man and must not be confused with the paramount purpose of his taking up residence here. In our enthusiasm to become, we must not trade away spiritual values and potentials for something of less worth. In eagerness to accomplish, we too often "worship the substance of things and ignore the maker." Only when we so refine the spirit that the soul becomes a moving force in reaching for the more lasting things of life, will there come a fullness of understanding as to why we are here.

Helen Keller said: "My darkness had been filled with the light of intelligence." From eyes that couldn't see emerged a light within her soul and she in her desire to grow, to be alive, did cultivate her spirit and determination to rise above the overruling absence of physical sight. Though the penetrating light of her soul, new worlds of thought and blessings came her way.

The gift of intelligence, given to every man, is an everlasting light that shines continually through the seasons. The light of day is dim and short lived compared to the brightness that is generated within the heart. "The glory of God is intelligence" and His spirit flows with glory through the stream of mankind, and whosoever desires may drink.

Miss Keller gained an inner glow to her identity, adding beauty to spirit that was beyond herself. Having lived the answers with a burning light within, she revealed her story and became the whole person. In her moments of perfection she lived near the Lord; never carrying the feeling of not being useful. In her restrictions she tried life and found it good. There were lonely days, but she was never alone. Her life ended in strength, and in memory she continues to live.

Many things that we in our 20-20 vision, have seen and wondered about, she understood.

HERE FOR A PURPOSE

We are not here in this phase of living to elbow one another out of the better seats, nor to keep score against one another. The purpose here is to build, to strengthen, and grow. We belong to the same team; made up of a like substance that is patterned from the same mold. The purpose isn't to fight evil with evil, but replacing the fallacies of life with lasting values.

Judas in his failure to reckon with the Lord, lost his state of credibility. He removed himself from the gospel team of the twelve apostles. And today as we face one another in our success and mistakes, we live among the unnumbered souls God has created in like model and style. We are copies of the Original that has never varied or changed during this continuous chain of living.

From the premortal assembly line of anxious spirits have come a perpetual flow of beautiful children to earth

live for the gift of happiness and the testing of dis-
appointments.

It's good to remember that in moments of weakness
when temptations come to do evil, the Lord remains on
standby to give us the higher choice of values to think
about. In accepting the light and truth we must be willing
to follow where it leads, and not only be alert to pitfalls,
but prepared to recognize and accept the best.

There is much goodness in this wicked world. Good
Samaritans everywhere are travelling the crowded high-
ways of life reaching out with that something special in
helping their fellowmen along the way. They bring peace
of mind to troubled hearts; bringing changes to their
lives.

The faith of Columbus overran his sight, but not the
field of vision. The pioneers had a well-defined vision to
come west before maps were made; in faith they made
their own. We are here to build up a working faith to carry
us across the chasm of rough going. We must be selective
in choices before us for we alone shape the soul to the
measure of things we have faith in. First and foremost is
faith in God and his Son Jesus Christ. They are the
fountainhead from which all truth flows through the
personage of the Holy Ghost. From this light of understanding the soul conditions itself to a new way of living
in keeping the heart content and the spirit on the move.

This day is the time of growth; the season of flowers,
the month of promise and a day for service. It's the hour
for giving and time for reflectoin of the things accomplished through the gift of time. We are building brick by
brick the house of faith and character of our thoughts in
which tomorrow we live.

As long as "mysterious gravity" keeps this confused world right side up, let's keep faith with the Lord.

HESITATION

The board of directors of a New York firm invited young Thomas A. Edison to a special meeting for the purpose of buying the patent on his newly invented "ticker tape" machine.

Before going to this important gathering, Edison decided that he would ask $3,000 for the invention, and if necessary, he would sell it for as little as $2,000.

He entered the board room and sat before the distinguished group. The chairman asked, "How much do you want for the patent?" For a moment Edison didn't know what to say; he hesitated. Before he could speak another member of the board broke the silence by saying, "regardless of what you may ask, we refuse to pay more than $40,000."

In a moment of having hesitated, a financial door opened to Mr. Edison and people everywhere have become recipients of his gifts and talent. He succeeded because he was a man of purpose who insisted on results, putting responsibility ahead of comfort; learning and unlearning facts about himself and scientific laws of the unknown. He made more opportunities than he found. He put the letter "P" in front of the word "luck" and soared to success in his chosen profession. Having taken advantage of daylight and most of nighttime hours, Mr. Edison spent more time with himself than anyone else. His inventions touched all points of life in adding years to the joy of living. "He took off his hat to the past and his coat to the future."

Many of Mr. Edison's experiments that turned out wrong surprised him by turning out right; never letting that which discouraged him, control him.

People came from everywhere to see his good works.

Each passing hour of our life is alive for action and decision making. There is something, however, that we must not delay or hesitate in doing, for undecided moments of the day soon add to years of lost time. To some, hesitation is merely a period of time reserved for indepth thinking, but in matters of life and salvation, a delay in opportunities designed for the growth of the soul is to lose it all for the soul cannot rise above the restriction that is placed on it by failure to act in the "now."

The cause for which man is placed here to do is bigger than himself.

IF

To feel the suspense and pressure of ball players in the final inning with the score tied and the bases loaded; or the intentness of a Quarterback playing on the losing side at the ten yard line, third down and five seconds to go; or the feel and excitement of spectators in the closing moments of a championship basketball game; until one feels such suspense and apprehension, only then will come the full impact and elation of being a participant in the cheering section of the winners, or among the dispirited and frustrated losers.

At various sporting events people gather to watch teams of their choice compete. When the contest ends, the most expressed comment is the word, "IF." How the game might have been played better.

So it is in the arena of living. We reflect how life may have been lived with greater acceptance and trust. It takes quality of mind to bear up under the burden of how things could have been. Having the willpower and courage to take defeat without losing heart is a winning effort.

The most important lesson we learn in the department of living is accepting the Lord's way of doing things. We, the performers, should live with "hammer and tong" vigorously and with conviction.

It has been said: "Sometimes it's good to have a few early loses in life to relieve the pressure of trying to keep intact an undefeated season." The greater victories come through having lost a game or two.

Nothing hurts in winning, but the pain of defeat teaches the greater lesson. A loss without accepting the challenge to try again is the highest order of defeat.

Every living day calls for a firmness of spirit and the will to do. There was a near perfect swimmer who lacked the courage to save a drowning man, and standing at his side was a fifty-percent swimmer with courage who dove in the water, and a life was saved. With his daring and determination, he took a calculated risk and became the perfect swimmer.

Having the courage to act and do with integrity of purpose is the overriding function of "living with a will." This we can do "if" we will. It's a quality that guarantees all others.

IN REVIEW

To live abundantly is the cause for which we are born; to die with respectability is the end to which we are dedicated. If today we are in harmony with things uplifting, tomorrow need have no fear. This phase of life's journey is too short and risky to be found doing things that are unacceptable to the Lord; things that get in our way such as the trouble makers of worry, hate, doubt, fear and sin.

My father assigned me and my three older brothers to weed a patch of sugar beets one morning as he left for his law practice in a small town in Idaho. He came home early that day and found two of us working on one side of the field and two on the other. As brothers we had a dispute over some minor issue and rather than fight we divided. He immediately put us all together again saying: "I didn't assign you this job to work apart, but work together." He had a long range view of what he wanted us to become.

It's Satan who spotlights and sets in motion the short range benefits, knowing that unorganized efforts of men relates to an organized state of unhappiness.

My father was more concerned with harmony of spirit; the art of getting along, than the weeds choking out the beets. He was aware that a small wedge divides and weakens.

Many lessons must be learned in bringing appreciation for the greater riches, things adding up to a state of joy and a satisfying life. Ideals and goodness of the heart rises and falls with our thoughts, for we become master or victims of life in the quality of our thinking. Having freedom of expression with a sense of responsibility is the only sound basis for happy days ahead.

The beauty of the rose has its season to bloom and the leaves their moments to fall, and we have this day to live. There is no joy that equals the feeling of peace that comes in the evening hour, knowing we have done our very best in making this life a more pleasant place to be.

We read about things of the past, but little do we know the pulsebeat and the atmosphere of the people making up the past. We can be sure their problems were as real and conflicting as our problems today, yet such events have their place. After all, a bed of roses isn't for evermore the best place to sleep, for its during palmy days when the soul has tendency to loaf and grow fat.

Every generation has had to settle problems on the basis of second best, as we today; yet, the noblest concept of man is knowing that in doing our very best, even though it may not be good enough, there follows a life beyond the shadow of this where the "Lord had declared the end from the beginning," and He'll be there where peace may come to the heart of many broken spirits.

IT BEGINS AND ENDS WITH YOU

Each day is a step forward on a continuous journey that is to last forever; it's home bound. The Gospel plan of life is a movement designed to enhance the spirit for a fullness in living. It's a force that to be seen must be felt. The prime time of life is reflected in that hour we become concerned with all life, just as seeds grow best in the soil that nourishes and brings all variety of flowers to full bloom.

To be successful in the business of living we must strengthen the resolve to be "rightly occupied" in the pursuit of the saving principles that contains the soul for a place of glory. The key in reaching a quality state of mind is the sharing of the seemingly little things. . .a pleasant smile, a thank you, and giving and leaving with others a part of ourselves.

The personality of man becomes enriched by making his wants fewer in accepting the more lasting treasures bound up in the spiritual aspect of living. Success and failure is the going business of the day which begins and ends with us. In learning well from mistakes, success presents no problems and delight rules the hour.

The unknown appointment for an accounting with the Lord is written on the calendar of time, and perhaps its coming will be sooner than we reckon, reminding us that the earthly things gathered are but a mere heartbeat away from being scattered, divided and entangled.

In reaching out while marching in tempo with the living words, "I am the way, the truth, and the light," is the hour we become most useful in dividing and sub-dividing our time with the Lord in adding glory to his name. It's a companionship arrangement with a promise. We are not the sole owners of life, but merely have a life's interest in it. The purpose of being here is to squander a little for the beautification of the soul.

Only as the windowpane and inner glow of the spirit becomes soiled and dirty will the flow of divine light be diverted and lose its power. Shadows of life conceals the man and the light of understanding reveals the person.

JOURNEY OF TRUST

As a youngster, while living on the farm, my father occasionally sent me to town with a signed blank check to purchase various items. He placed trust and confidence in me that over his signature I would fill out the check properly. Upon arriving home an account was called for to balance the items purchased with the amount the check was made out for.

This life is a journey of responsibility in which the character of man is measured in the way he responds to assignments. His behavior must be accounted for and balanced out against the things he knew to be right and wrong.

The honor and respect we extend the Lord is in relation to the way we treat our fellowmen. No person can truly love God and mistreat his neighbors, or give glory to Him and ignore the mission of His Son Jesus, nor can one keep in touch with the Lord if he's out of touch with the sick and downtrodden.

The Lord is the power of our existence and the source of our strength. Failure to accept his teachings cuts the main line of supply and dims the light that feeds the soul. Things good and uplifting relate to intelligent growth, anything less retards the spirit. Those holding positions of responsibility, and trust receive public attention. They are in the limelight, with a spotlight revealing their strength and weakness. The greatest reward isn't when one gets his name in "Who's Who" or elected president or governor. Greatness is attained in the degree one becomes Godlike. Only then is living totally successful.

Man's greatest work lies beyond his minimum effort, and we are here, not by chance but by choice, coming from a spiritual setting of activity in premortal living.

JUDGMENT DAY

On May 19, 1780, there came a total eclipse of the sun at Hartford, Connecticut. The State Legislature was then in session when the eclipse and darkness came. It was noontime. The meeting of the Lower House broke up in alarm. In the Senate a motion of adjournment was made so the legislators could meet the Day of Judgment. The motion was opposed by Abraham Davenport, a Yankee Selectman and Judge, friend and advisor of George Washington. He arose and addressed his legislative colleagues. "I am against this adjournment," he said, "The Day of Judgment is either approaching or it is not, there is no cause of adjournment. If it is, I choose to be found doing my duty. I wish, therefore, that candles may be brought."

The Day of Judgment may stir the minds of men, but when it comes, the hour is passed to change direction. As the final judgment appears on the horizon there is no escape, no time to enter into a "Noah's Ark," shut the door, and ride out the flood.

We may have days when it is ill-lighted and overcast, but way out yonder the sun continues to shine. A judgment may clarify destination, but it never changes what we are.

We must have quality of trust in the struggle to live and dare to move forward. In the midst of extreme trouble and rebellion, Columbus recorded: "This day we sailed on course." It's through the power of faith that transforms doubt into new discoveries, reminding us that the point of contact with life in which we find ourselves is where our thoughts have taken us.

"We must not confuse the person we are with the person we were or the person we will become," but we should continually reach for new horizons, lest the sun sets in our life at noonday.

The events making up the quiet past are of the same substance as those making headlines in the stormy present. The balance of living comes when we touch life at all points in building integrity of purpose while reaching beyond our grasp for higher values.

"We can't control nature, the wind or the tide, but we can control ourselves in patience, giving the wind and tide a chance to change."

All clocks must be regulated to the master timepiece of the universe if meaningful and stability of order is to be calculated for the blessing of man, yet most important is regulating the mechanism and delicate timepiece of the spirit to the pulsebeat of the Lord. We are His creation and his most valued possession; yet we are classified as the most far distance from perfection.

It is obvious that we are all serving time under a suspended sentence, waiting the call of destiny from which judgment will come.

LAW

Soil, making up the surface layer of the earth, supports all life. It's for cultivation and production of food to sustain man. Dirt is filth, something swept up from the floor. It has no life sustaining values, yet man in his desires for the sensational aspects of living has learned to sweep filth and grime into the mind of others, bringing to the world an overpopulation of degenerate characters. Within our grasp, we can reach and choose the best or second best.

Men in their deceptive behavior are merely good people gone wrong; just as darkness is the absence of light and love unrelated to hate. All people were good people in the beginning.

The more we seek to learn of ourselves, the less pleased we are of what we find in ourselves. Should the Lord permit us to catch a glimpse of our spiritual rating on his divine scale of measurements, would we be happy with what we saw?

We are dependent creatures, citizens of life bound up by the ground rules of the universe. We alone in our weakness cannot save ourselves, nor alone find ourselves. A higher power must come to sustain, to fulfill, to give direction and meaning to life's unfinished struggle.

During the encounter with living, men are encompassed with supreme laws, laws that cannot be changed—only broken. The laws of God bind the Creator to his creations, to the promises that encircle his powers. To freely move within the circle of His divine power and authority is to have almost beheld the glory of God and remained in the flesh.

Man is too often seen as he appears to be, rather than the potentials of his hidden powers to become. Those concealed talents are untainted, unspotted and refined, alive and ready to fulfill their call to responsibility. Man must condition his life to the law of obedience in bringing to the surface the richness of those powers and talents that are sheltered within.

Readiness for death is not related to power or position. It is developed through love and sharing with others. Maturity of responsibility will clarify itself by the manner in which the journey of choices were made and the application of love we infused into the lives of others.

There may be many unanswered prayers as we leave mortality, that may be carried directly to the Lord in person, in the next estate, for an evaluation of content to be listened to and acted upon.

No greater concussion to the spirit will equal the shock in not being accepted into our Father's presence, and there will be no joy equal to that of receiving a fullness of His glory.

It takes little thought to discover that the supply of truth is more in abundance, waiting to be used, than a demand for its use.

As the dust settles from a life having been used up, perhaps the "no" answers to our prayers will be more blessed and effective to our state of glory than the "yes" answers.

LIFE IN MOTION

In the revolutionary war with England in 1776, leaders of America won their freedom fighting against their fathers. In the Civil War of 1861-65, the armies of the north conquered the south fighting their brothers, cousins and neighbors. And, today we are continually at war with ourselves, hoping to win a victory over that rebellious spirit within. We are a combination of strength and weakness and must consider the end with the beginning in disciplining ourselves for a place of tranquility in the realm of happiness.

The battle of life goes on; in the sky and beneath the sea. Near the bottom of the ocean, the Torpedo, or Electric Ray fish, remains motionless, waiting for its favorite meal to pass by. As the Crab nears, the fish sends out an electric volt that stuns the Crab, and a meal is eaten leisurely.

From the sky the Hawk is a constant challenge to the rodents and other life beneath.

There is mystery in death and adventure in living, yet without the open road of death, life would become dull and never-ending with no incentive to challenge the spirit for a place of nobility in the royal kingdom.

The ocean tide has its ups and downs. All nature is on the move; and behind all life is design and purpose. The best of most jobs are yet to be started and the finest work of our labors awaits to be finished. We are made up of an earth-bound body and a glory-bound spirit.

Six days of the week is the battleground on which the issues of life are fought. The seventh, the Sabbath, is the day of truce, bringing a cease fire to the soul; a time to pause and refresh; to mellow and recover. It's a special day, along with the other six, in which the Lord reveals the excellence of his work, the greatness of his glory and the purpose of our coming this way.

This is our day to identify with the world the best within we have to offer. Having an inward peace is the greatest sought after blessing. It's an enriched treasure that brings wealth to the mind and happiness to the soul.

If there is to be a harvest beyond today, it's a miscalculation to be stingy with the seeds planted in the present.

LIVING AMONG US

Living among us is an individual with power that never quits; he's real and alive, and has a scorched-earth policy to destroy you and me. This person ignores things past. He concentrates on the present with intent to scuttle the future in his gamble for high stakes—the souls of men. Never helping anyone out of trouble, he is very selective with whom he associates, ignoring people who are unclean, the corrupt and those living in open shame of broken laws. This segment of society is already his own.

Never leaving the scene of the crime, all things destructive are justified in his eyes. In his world-wide operations he is enemy number one. His personality is past recovery and redemption. He's the Devil and rejoices when the spirit and flesh unites in a venture of self-disintegration.

We are Satan's best helpers. We write degrading books that youth read and produce the shows they see. We distill the liquor they drink and grow the poisonous plants they consume. We originate corrupt stories that taints the soul and style the clothes they wear.

The Lord's non-intervention of evil in human affairs isn't a sign of his absence and unconcern for us, but through agency of choice, it reveals that we are "ever learning and never able to come to a knowledge of the truth" . . .a light of understanding that comes only through a "quickening of intelligence to keener perceptions of things spiritual."

In this competitive way of life there are few men who have the strength to withstand the offer of the highest bidder.

Satan's finest weapon to discredit the soul of man is through distortion of truth. Deception is the point of beginning that corrodes and narrows the flow of spiritual awakenings. It brings a deficiency of character that must be overcome if there is to be joy and fulfillment to living.

If the downbeat of our tempo is in step with the ways of the world, we are out of touch with life and the concept, that "man is that he might have joy." Joy is the overflow of happiness that emerges from living the Lord's way of doing things; a sustaining truth that develops the total person.

From birth unto death, from sunrise to sunset, is a measurable interval of time in which we become what we are cast to be, through our choice to become.

MAKING THE MOST

As we are caught up in the stream of life, the question unfolds: Will we, or will we not turn in a "top flight" performance? Being captains of our ship, we set the sail; stand at the helm and control the rudder; making a choice of the course taken.

Man is the central figure of the universe; having been endowed with a command of excellence in doing worthy deeds and things useful for a place in the kingdom.

The challenge of man is knowing who he is, where he stands, and the potential of his becoming.

Living among us are loyal and dedicated people who have turned in "top flight" performance; reaching a special place of satisfaction with the Lord.

Jesus of Nazareth set the example and leads the parade. He's at the top. His mission is the first and foremost perfected work in human history. His atoning sacrifice is unequaled in the promise of life eternal and a place of glory in the heavens. This gift of life after death, became the Savior's supreme and final act in mortality before the curtain fell.

Jesus was not an economist, a lawyer, a scientist nor an engineer by trade. He was a builder of men, a carpenter who carved out the blue prints and the know-how for all manner of men to follow in reaching the top in their chosen line of work.

A ten billion dollar a year business, operating today was founded at Kemmerer, Wyoming, in 1902, on the principle of the "Golden Rule." James Cash Penny was a profound student of life and understood the related value of the Savior's mission to the needs of the business world. The pieces of life are here to be recognized and put together where values fit best. The Lord provided the platform, the "Golden Rule" from which J. C. Penny launched his selling program.

"The most interesting game in the world is making the most of our best." One of the less difficult things in life is to finish the course without having left any trace of passing this way. A person is measured more by the quality of his life than the scale of his living. There is need to challenge the meaning and purpose of being here, lest we wander at large in a cycle of confusion.

We cannot escape one another even though we travel at different level of circumstances. An ocean liner is usually built with three decks; consisting of the upper, middle and lower. If such a ship hits an iceberg, suddenly all the people aboard realize they are on the same boat. In an instant there is no distinction of rank and title. All are equal and unclassified and life becomes precious and real. It is then they must close ranks to a common cause of living or dying together.

MEASURING ROD

Professor Clement C. Moore, married at the age of thirty-five, was asked by his children a few years later, to tell them a Christmas story. He, being a very meticulous and exacting person, wrote a poem especially for them which he read during the Yule season. The poem carried the title, "'Twas the Night Before Christmas."

Harriet Butler, a visiting friend in the home, saw the poem and was given a copy, the use of which was intended for her only. Later, Dr. Moore saw the poem in a local newspaper, and even though his name was not attached as the author, he became very upset. He had written a fairy tale as a "fun thing" for his children, not something for public use and didn't wish to expose himself as having dabbled in writing about things unreal.

Professor Moore had been a teacher in a Biblical Theological Seminary in New York, and in 1814, he was then a full Professor of Oriental and Greek Literature and had compiled the first Hebrew dictionary in the United States. He had learned every language. With his high credentials he didn't want to be humiliated and embarrassed by his collegues and intellectual associates by letting it be known that his gifted pen had been guilty of writing such a flipant bit of make-believe. To him it would be out of context and taint his dignity.

He remained silent for fifteen years, and then the story got out. In 1839 he admitted that he had written the poem and was guilty of this deception.

Dr. Moore is best known today through this make-believe spin-off piece of writing, yet his greater satisfaction at the time came from the reputation of his indepth works as a literary scholar. He was pleased with the praise and plaudits received from his fellow intellectuals. It has been said that "fame is merely the spirit of man that survives itself in the minds and thoughts of others."

Although Professor Moore lived and worked among the learned, his highest measure of return evolved from the hearts of children. He had caught the fancy of their young minds and passed it along in his writing. They came alive to a wider horizon of thought and dreams. Imagination is the frame-work in which children live, and what he wrote as a passing interest, remains today as the most widely read of his works. His success came in the happiness he gave to others, extending itself with every new birth.

What is the measure of success? C. S. Lewis has written: "Unless a measuring rod is independent of things measured, we can do no measuring." Dr. Moore unknowingly pinpointed his measurement of success with the younger generation through the fantasies and vision of sugar plums and rainbows in the sky. This attainment came as an afterbeat to his intellectual accomplishments.

Elements of truth are unchangeable and are fixed rules of measurement; it's the yardstick by which dimensions of life are balanced and brought into perspective. Understanding the laws of truth becomes the prime mover of all that is good.

Very often that which is pursued becomes secondary to that which is discovered. The moments Dr. Moore spent in writing " 'Twas the Night Before Christmas" are rich moments in the hearts of young people everywhere. In the great "book of life" young inquiring minds are listed as the "pure in heart" among the elect of the Lord's kingdom.

We measure best ourselves in the hearts of little children in the things that bring them happiness. They live in their own little world of discovery, living independent with things real to them.

" 'Twas the Night Before Christmas" lives on.

MEETING THE CHALLENGE

In meeting the challenge to improve and grow with the seasons, it is soon learned that it takes more application of thought and know-how to do certain things right the first time than on the second attempt. It takes less attention and time to make the second dress than the first. The nature of the challenge hasn't changed; only the ability and skill in meeting the challenge has come into its own.

In the beginning God put the breath of life into man and he became a living soul. This was the point of beginning in the rise and fall of man in mortality.

Through the revolving door of death, to a state of resurrection, is merely another step forward in the plan of life and salvation. To live again in body and spirit, is a repeat performance by the Lord in the application of the same divine principles used in the creation.

The outlined plan for reaching a state of perfection is the greatest set of blueprints ever devised for the glory of man. The Lord is very selective among those coming back into his presence. There are restrictions. No unclean thing will get through. Hypocrites won't make it. Unless man is born of water and of the spirit he hasn't a chance. Failure to visit the sick, feed the hungry, and clothe the naked never enhances ones position of qualification to pass through the gate.

Narrow is the way leading to the "hall of fame" in the glory of celestial living. Satan never participated in the creations of life...we owe him nothing, but that which we are and hope to become, we are indebted to the Lord.

The knowledge of truth must be lived to possess it, yet we can't liberate that which hasn't been captured. Until we capture the love of God, in whose image we are created, the truth will never liberate and set us free.

Before coming to this life we pre-assessed things here that would be hostile and blind us to a more delightful state of living, but knowing the risk was high, we took a chance and made a choice. As we live in this time-frame of mortal existence, there isn't time to discover all truth; it must be revealed.

MEMORIES THROUGH MUSIC

A most uplifting and rewarding gift that touches the life of man is through the flow of music. . .it mellows the soul and controls the hour, becoming the natural outlet of self-expression and group participation. As melodies grow older, they become richer in memory, bringing joy to living. Someone has written that "music is the harmonious voice of creation, it's an echo of the invisible world. . .it calms the soul and is one of the most delightful presents God has given to us."

Surely life would be a misstep without the sound of music. Concerning Christmas it would lose a part of its glory by reason that Jesus was ushered into life with a song as "the angels and heavenly hosts sang praise to a new born child and gave glory to God." With harmony of purpose angels from above revealed in song a New Beginning, and as we sing songs of happiness at Christmastime, the pulse beat of many hearts ascends in harmony heavenward to blend in with the great plan of life and salvation.

When words leave off, music begins and without it to enhance the joy of living, life would be a mistake.

It would seem unthinkable to have the old year end and the new move in without ringing bells, and the blast of trumpets. Melody with a beat has away of lifting the spirits of men. A soldier was asked why he joined the army. He replied: "I signed up while the band was playing." The strains of music has a message for every occasion. . ." it is heard over the field of battle; men lie dying with it in their heart. . .it calls the wanderer back home and it opens the lips of lovers." Many souls are touched as music "tells the story of love and a message that saves and a story that damns."

A beautiful song has the power to bring joy to the heart of one person, while to another it brings sadness to the soul, just as "the same sun that hardens the clay softens the wax."

Music is "close to the marriage alter, and near the open grave." Shakespeare has written: "Why was music ordained? Was it not to refresh the mind of man after his studies, or his usual pain?" When the harmony of things about us are admitted to the soul, there evolves a spiritual feeling that remains and never dies.

L. E. Landon has written that "music moves us, and we know not why; we feel the tears, but cannot trace their source. Is it the language of some other place brought back in memory? For what can wake the soul's strong instinct of another world like music?"

As meadowlarks sing, my thoughts recall memories of youth, reflecting on the pleasant hours while taking the dairy herd to the river pasture. The killdeer and other song birds thrilled me as a lad, yet we can never return again in person to the era of our childhood, but with the speed of light there comes many returns in memory to those carefree days.

As melody of songs echo among the birds. . .the insects of the field; through trees and rippling streams, there comes the feeling that life is beautiful, and as long as the melodic sound of music prevails, hope remains that mankind will succeed.

MOTHERS

Mothers are special people with inherent gifts of bringing life to the world. They are chosen of the Lord, fulfilling the highest position of honor in mortality through the divine capacity and unique power of creation; bringing organized bodies from the dust of the earth, a dust with distinct characteristics that has mixed so well with the spirit; a creation identified as a soul, a combination of spirit and clay that carries a name.

Fulfilling her divine calling, a mother unfolds an exacting role; a distinction extending beyond the calculation of time. No replacement has evolved that can substitute for her place of responsibility in the home. She is the centerpiece of love and effectiveness in teaching her children the pathway to the riches of eternity.

It has been said that a small boy coming into the house, and seeing only Dad and the other children, with mother missing, expressed his true feelings when he said:

"Where's everybody." A child was asked the question: "Where is home?" The reply came, "where mother is." The clock stops in the heart of a child when mother is absent. . .she is his total life. Children choose friends, but mother stands at the top of the list in bringing fulfillment to their needs. She is the morning and evening hour in the home, with a sustained overflow of spiritual influence for the blessings and building of family life. When help is needed, she's there on time with that special "something" that only she can give. Her presence creates the atmosphere for living success; having that inborn aptitude for placing priority on needs of the family over her own comfort and convenience. Yet there are those living among us who insist that we vote women as being equal in structure and physical unlikeness as men, while others oppose having women, the mothers of all men, with their singular touch of femininity, descend to this level.

Why is it that she, the "elect" of the Lord, in her dedicated calling so willingly gives so much for her children, leaving so little time for herself? The answer was predetermined at the council of the creation in heaven. It's because she's a mother, "the queen of the home," a person of inexhaustable love; a symbol of all that is right and reassuring in the world.

NEED OF DIRECTION

There was a young lad trying to lead a large dog. He was asked: "Where are you taking the dog?" He replied: "I'm waiting to see which direction he wants to go, then I'll take him there."

Some folks have that built-in tendency of letting circumstances set the direction they take. Many ships have wrecked because "the pilot chose the wrong beacon." The north star relates the position of man to the rest of the universe. There are many roads to every life that extends beyond the sunset and there's a "right step" that leads to a glory that goes on forever. The most important, from birth unto death, on this one direction course, is the step that meets the other person half-way.

The wind picks up the fallen leaf and whirles it into motion, seemingly without design or purpose, yet the seasons producing the leaf are constant, never failing in bringing a variety of gifts for the blessing of man.

The laws of nature are the approved laws of the Lord.

The past continually speaks into the present. As seeds are sown, followed by cultivatoin, there emerges a crop. The apples on the tree relate to the fallen blossoms just as the brotherhood between man and mother-earth remain in effect. The basic principles of living haven't changed since the Lord said "Cursed is the ground for thy sake." The blessing of the "curse" is binding and keeps a meaningful balance between man and reality. We are part of the soil and must cultivate it to keep it. Work may be troublesome, but it isn't damnation; it's a force that fashions and shapes destiny. The soul is enhanced through the blessing of use, giving life a pleasant journey.

There isn't a specified road to the Kingdom of God, the Kingdom is the road, but there is a way and Jesus spelled it out in the words of expression to his Father: "Thy will be done."

Humility must take us by the hand before we truly arrive in the kingdom of high adventure.

NEIGHBORS

A lady of wealth visited another person who was then living in reduced circumstances. Inquiry was made if she could bring her some food and other needed items for the home. Proudly the answer came that she didn't want charity. During the visit another women entered the open door with food and other necessities. They were accepted with appreciation by the lady in need. The well-to-do person asked why her help was refused and the answer came: "She's my neighbor."

Neighbors are special. They live in their own little world of friends and carry that singular touch of kindness with feelings of concern; living within calling distance, in the same environment and speaking the same language. Their visits in the neighborhood bring joy to the day; filling vacant places in the heart.

Good neighbors are those who feel free in the presence of one another; accepting things the way they are; having time enough to listen, with love enough to care and the patience to understand.

The things we do in life may be questioned; what is said may be challenged and expressions of thought may be misunderstood, but giving a helping hand to those in need is something special that is understood in any language. What we do with what we have where we are is the index indicating where values are placed. Walking with dignity of purpose while easing the overload of others, is most desirable; it's the place where duty would have us be at a given moment.

The greatest time of growth comes with steps taken beyond the realm of the first mile; a journey that's worth all the rest. It's a forever feeling of joy in the heart that comes only from things spiritual within.

"We like people in the proportion to the good we do them not what they do for us."

Neighbors are home made in the things we do to make them happy and in the process of doing, the greater joy comes to us.

NOTHING HAPPENS

It has been written that in the month of February 1809, down in Hardin County Kentucky, two back wood farmers met on the country road. One farmer asked his friend, "Is there any news down in the village, Ezra?" "Yes," he replied, "the storekeeper, McHale, has gone to Washington to see Madison sworn in as President of our country, and a Mr. Taylor who is at the print shop tells me this Napoleon Bonaparte feller has captured most of Spain."

"What's the news out your way, Henry?" "Nothing at all; nothing at all, except a new babe was born down to

Tom Lincoln's place the other night. They named him 'Abraham' and they're going to call him 'Abe' for short. No sir, nothing ever happens out here."

With the arrival of every new born babe something special has happened. A new born child, in the eyes of the Lord, whether it be a Lincoln, a Washington, a Churchill, or whether it be a member of the "rank and file", or in the class of the "unwanted," is special. Every living person is a spiritual off-spring of God and is important to His program in bringing "to pass the immortality and eternal life of man."

The greatest law of creation is fulfilled with every new born child through the law of continuation. Without birth there can be no death, no resurrection, and no exaltation. Without exaltation to the higher kingdom, there would be no candidates in training preparing to become as God is, to stand at the head of one of the many planets that He has organized for the celestial family of man.

The Lord said: "Worlds without number have I created, and by the Son I created them, the heavens they are many and they cannot be numbered into man, but they are numbered unto me for they are mine. For behold this is my work and glory to bring to pass the immortality and eternal life of man." Moses 1:33, 37-39.

Man is the purpose for which "worlds without number" have been organized and set in motion.

The noble and humble men of the earth, the pure in heart, are not born to greatness. . .they ascend to their positions of glory through the law of growth and obedience. In simplicity, many students of life move up to a high place among men, quietly and without fanfare, fulfilling and giving of themselves, doing preeminent work, unnoticed, quietly and fulfilling, just as the sun ripens the tomatoes in my back yard, as if it had nothing else to do.

ON THE INSIDE

In the year 1865 there was born a child with a crooked leg. He was disfigured, having a lump on his back. He was a brilliant youngster. At seven he learned Greek and at eight had a respectable knowledge of algebra and geometry. At ten he was ready to graduate from the school he attended.

Through the help of a well-to-do friend he made his way to America. He limped up the busy streets of New York and entered the Edison Electric Company and applied for a job. The chief engineer gave a firm refusal in the words: "There are too many engineers coming to America these days." A few days later he found the job he sought with another firm.

It was in January 1892 that the American Institute of Electrical Engineers of America met to see if they could solve the big problem of calculating the power and efficiency of generators while in the process of building them. Using alternating current there was an unknown loss of energy to be measured and accounted for. Up to that point the engines were built blindly as to their exact efficiency. It had been a hit-and-miss operation... "build first and then see how it works."

As this meeting came near its close, with nothing revealed that solved the mystery, a young man raised his hand and asked to speak. He walked to the platform in his crippled condition, and began to read from his prepared paper in broken English.

The crowd was restless. . .what could this unknown engineer have to offer? Charles Steinmetz was his name. He took command. In his crippled body he stood tall. Within minutes the group sat up and began to listen intently as he read his mathematical paper calculating the loss of energy. The character of his thoughts on electrical science was so luminous his physical features went unnoticed. They were amazed with his indepth presentation.

A mathematical genius was at work. In his paper he formulated, definitely and for all time, the exact law of Hystersis, a law that explained in detail the lag in changes of magnetization behind the varying magnetizing forces. His formula tamed electricity to the needs of man. Steinmetz was no longer a German "Alien;" he was an American forerunner. This group of Engineers had been looking for a leader to direct their course to a promised land of scientific achievement. Steinmetz reached beyond his grasp and became their answer, presenting them with three volumnes of complicated equations.

Knowledge and desire is the first step to great undertakings. A scientist soon learns to walk humbly before a fact, and will trample an untruth beneath his feet. This man with scientific know-how discovered a formula and adapted his thinking to follow where it led; staying within the bounds of law and order, never forcing an answer.

Living among us are those who are weak in body but strong with intellectual understanding. Regardless of the status quo of our position in mortality, weak or strong, every person in the fleet of mankind has an exacting work to do in reaching a place of reknown among men.

We often march to the beat of a different drummer, but parades soon pass and we must set the tempo to our own music and bring to the surface the best there is to offer. And when we are willing and ready, the call will be there to use us.

We may not be a Steinmetz but we are a person. He was suppressed as a child before he became a man, and was an individual of integrity before he became a scientist. Refusing to leave his talents undiscovered, he earned the right to praise himself; yet there was little need, others became his voice.

ON THE SPOT TRAINING

Life may not bring fulfillment to the demands we make of it, but with patience and a dash of common sense, the gift of this day will satisfy the demands we make of ourselves.

In attempts to better conditions we may falter and stumble in seeking desirable things; yet, in deficiencies and mistakes we remain uppermost among the creations of the Lord. We stand at the top of the list, with unlimited potential, operating in a special biological classification. As children of the Lord, there awaits an overflow of conditional blessings based on faith, shaped by love and added upon by the penetration of truth of which the world knows so little about so much.

There is an unending cycle of association between youth and age; it's a partnership arrangement. Age is looked to for having wisdom and concern for the young, leaving them bridges of understanding to pass over; while youth in their seeking for acceptance and approval, struggle in the "test-tube" of learning. They live in the present with hope and anticipation; while age seek guarantees and the shelter of security. Young people live for the hour as they seek out their day, while age lives for the day as they measure their years.

Life is a continued story, a narration of events that moves into many settings. It is unlike a book with beginning and ending; unlike something finished within the limits of time. The adventures of this excursion is made up of many written and untold stories, many of which go to press before proofs are read and contents of the script edited and evaluated.

The accumulation of worldly goods will, in the end, be the lesser part of our holdings. The mistakes and irresponsibility of purpose for the better life are cast to bring a state of distress and complication when the "flash-backs" of mistakes are seen passing in review. This laboratory of learning is a place for "on the spot" training, a testing ground revealing how the challenge was met in meeting head on with high failure and low success.

OUR PLACE IN THE WORLD

The smallest grain of sand is bound up with the entire solar system of planet earth. This small particle may bury itself and change size and form, but it can never escape from that to which it belongs.

This rotating world of ours is a part of a circle system of other planets that revolves about the sun and is subject to the law that relates to all heavenly bodies.

John Burrough says: "This earth has no underside or upperside. You can go from north to south; east to west, and you find no bottom. Go out into space and there is no up or down, no east or west. There is no sense of motion because there is no fixed position of something not in motion."

The Lord is the fixed point from which we chart our course. The promised riches descending from above relates to perfect order of law that will rise again. The attempt to restrict talent and functions of responsibility limits the potential of reaching the highest condition of excellence. The seeds of love and inspiration planted in the hearts of men seeking the greater light, keep pushing up and up in meeting the challenge of unfolding events of time; seeds designed to bloom in high places in the hour of their greatest need.

Day and night are intervals that measure the flow of time, just as the light of truth and darkness of indifference determines the destiny of man. We need the qualities and fixed points of stability of one another as we reach out beyond ourselves. The beauty of the soul is expressed in uplifting thoughts we receive from the heart of friends. Beyond this promised hour, we live and become alive only in doing those things of higher values that challenge the best in us.

The heart is never deceived...it tells a story the way it is. What comes tomorrow depends mostly on what we have done with the gifts of today, and this could be a quality year as we seek to develop our best to pass along to the best in others.

History claims our past but we command the present for a season as special guests of earth life. We are but a small grain of sand with a soul that is reaching for a place in the treasure-house of eternity.

We on this revolving planet are a part of the "solar-system" in the family of man.

OVERCOMING

Overcoming obstacles become one of the major victories of life. We dread tragedy; we abhor and deplore it. Yet there is nothing we admire more than the person who handles it triumphantly. There is nothing quite so picturesque and revealing as the qualities and characteristics making up the personality that classifies the real person.

Pain and sorrow afflicting man are most impressive teachers; but seldom do we let the events of passing pleasure teach us anything.

Lincoln not only endured tragedies; he built character out of them; while in the life of King Saul, he revealed qualities that are seen in the best of the human family, and also the weakness and frailities in the worst of mankind.

When we live the answers to the more difficult questions of life, we confirm the validity and purpose of living. Only as we live the answers to things uplifting do we filter from the mind deceptive and unrelated things in reaching for things that add joy to living. To exhaust our capabilities in becoming a better person is to have caught the vision and purpose of which we are created. Opportunities to do lofty deeds may never come, but to do common everyday acts of kindness are with us daily.

Many things we encounter are hard to bear and usually more difficult to understand, yet we delight in seeing that person who zeros in with enthusiasm on the spiritual and uplifting aspects of living.

The purpose of life; of living; of education is finding ourself as an individual; becoming anxiously engaged in doing something more useful than the accumulation of perishable goods.

It was intended that we attain in this life our full capacity as a person. We are judged from results; not intentions. Effectiveness will not exceed preparation.

As we move through cycles of living, our mistakes become most impressive teachers, and as we meet them head on, face to face, their lessons must be accepted and controlled or we perish.

A small pipe laid parallel at the edge of a running stream will carry its proportionate power and force of the river towards destination. As we parallel our thinking to the things of the Lord, our spiritual intake receives the high tide of divine guidance; the use of which brings an overflow of joy to the heart; filling the reservoir of love to the breaking point.

OVERFLOW

In seeking out a life of happiness we sometimes fail to recognize the element that generates happiness. Wasted days and too much leisure time curtails the flow of things that bring joy to living. Having an overflow of worldly possessions are deceptive in relationship to a state of happiness.

People who are considered as the "salt of the earth" are not necessarily those with an oversupply of earthly accumulations, who believe they have out maneuvered, out fought, and out died those having operated with so little. The elect among men are those who have stability of purpose; having stood the test in behavior and concern for the less fortunate, recognizing values that bring a balanced innerglow to life.

Passing the "salt test" is keeping alive the savor of uplifting thoughts while enriching and bringing useful changes into the lives of others.

According to Ralph W. Seager, the Lord has given us "more sky than we can see, more sea than we can sail, more sun than we can bear, more stars than we can count, more air than we can breathe, more harvest than we sow and more love than we can know."

The gifts of life are here in abundance for the joy of its taking and if we fail to receive, we are not reaching out. The lack of success in being a real person is failure altogether, for this place of action is serious business . . .we are here that we "might have joy," making this journey a place of high adventure where it's better to have written our name in the register of the Lord than recording it in the best journals of men.

This day is an extension of yesterday reminding us that the hour is at hand where knowledge must give way to understanding if the joy of living is to come into its own. During this one-direction course of living we generate an immense sum of useless trouble that diverts attention to that which brings sorrow to our lives, and perhaps the greatest loss in making the most of our intellectual capacity to think, is the love we never gave and the power we never used in making this place a more inviting schoolroom of learning.

Our real treasures are family and friends, and we being the forerunners of those who follow, must set the pace to keep alive the soundness of moral principles that unfolds through righteous living.

Each of us have a heritage and birthright that we either build upon or diminish, and failure in knowing who our foreparents are is pathetic and unreal, but to forget them is sad indeed.

PASSING MOMENTS

One of the far reaching statements to challenge and strengthen the inner workings of the spirit was introduced to the world in the 19th century. It is recorded: "As man now is God once was, and as God is man may be."

To reach this God-like position of intelligence becomes a continuous process that calls for pure love and undeviating strength in being obedient to the laws of heaven upon which all "blessings are predicated."

Satan has knowledge and power, but in his nefarious schemes in getting men "to worship him," has compressed his spirit and agency to a state of perdition. In deception he lacked the application of knowledge to comply with truth, and became the devil.

"From dust thou art" combined with the spirit, has mixed so well in the formation of man, that hopefully this combination will find its way to a place of glory in the kingdom of our Father. We must have agency of choice for the greater gifts offered by the Lord for the right to dwell in His presence.

A most important question may be asked at the judgment seat, "did you feed the hungry, clothe the naked, and visit the sick?" Giving service to lighten the load of others is quite easy, yet very exacting. It's a mark of compassion and love for the more lasting treasures of life eternal.

Jesus learned all about earth life—he's been here before and understands problems of hunger, disease and death. His atoning mission for the mistakes of men is complete. He restored, enhanced and gave life new meaning, setting in order things that have been and things "hidden before the foundation of the world."

We must not only prevail but overcome. The measure of progress and balance of understanding revealing integrity of character are seen in the degree of tolerance and reservation of judgment we have toward our fellow associates, those who differ with us on the subjects of politics, creed and complexion.

The hour of peace comes in that moment we harmonize eternal law to personal situations, where with dignity we charge the "write-off" of mistakes as growth factors in gaining new experiences in reaching out for progressive values.

Dwelling in our Father's kingdom is where only the best is good enough.

POWER OF THE SPIRIT

The power of the Holy Ghost, the gift of the spirit, is the means by which God communicates his will and message to the hearts of men.

Through this power man receives a 20-20 vision in the light and understanding of the truth. The craftiness of men cannot divert this penetrating spirit. It led Columbus to the shores of America. Saul of Tarsus received the message and was born again to change his name to "Paul the Missionary." It's a moving force by which the Lord gets his work going on earth. The power of the Holy Spirit is available to everyone who desires to be a better person; those seeking for greater knowledge and truth, in building and reaching for the guiding hand of the Lord.

We live in a special time of life; the dispensation of the fullness of times. An era that embraces all the powers, keys, privileges of past divine administrations. Into our day have all dispensations emerged. It began with Adam heading up the family of man. It has moved into the 19th century with all its glory through the guiding hands of Joseph Smith, a prophet of the Lord.

Every father and mother stand at the head of a family dispensation. They have a love that only they can give. Their role is to dispense, administer and manage affairs by the authority, promises and principles made under the marriage covenant. This is their day in the "fullness of times" to administer, to teach and share in building a faith unto good works. It's a family dispensation. . .a harvest time of souls.

It's one thing having the ability to produce a family, but quite another to provide for their needs; keeping them sustained with spiritual nourishment for a quality life; reinforcing souls for a place in the kingdom. Too often we find ourselves in enemy-occupied territory where Satan has built a fortress.

The gift of the spirit is needed to shatter the steel walls of neglect and indifference.

Overcoming the ways of the world and correcting mistakes is the stimulus that brings growth and understanding to the heart of man. The field of involvement for greater blessings is before us to be challenged. Choices are many and varied in things to be done. Now is the hour of decision.

There are gardens to plant, to cultivate, and the harvest to gather. Children are yet unborn. Lives are to be lived and there are homes to be built. Lessons are to be taught and stories are waiting to be told. Problems of the day must be solved without multiplying the risk of creating greater ones. As the world turns, a salvation must be earned for this day on earth will end. When this facet of living has passed, it adds up to a moment only of living time in the schedule of the Lord.

Today's best security is finding us doing our best, yet this may not be good enough. . .our best may be failure; we must do what is necessary.

PREPARATION

Before opportunity can be seized with any degree of assurance, there must come preparation to meet the challenge. It emerges from the fruits of thought and labor of prepared minds. In its formation period the opportune moment isn't something that turns up; it's something that's dug up. Opportunity must not only be seen, but recognized.

Man is the means and the vehicle through which the riches of life forever moves and runs its course. New adventures become lost and helpless without enthusiastic seekers, yet the door opens when the knock is heard.

Opportunity carries no letter of introduction. We must interject and make the first move for it takes many years of understudy and dedicated training to recognize spiritual values of permanence and integrity of purpose.

It was Jesus, our Lord and Savior, whose divine mission became known overnight plus thirty-three years of intensive training. Kaltenborn became a celebrated public figure in broadcasting in eighteen days plus twenty years in getting ready for that timely moment. Charles A. Lindberg, age twenty-five, was just another name in the phone book on May 20, 1927. Thirty-three and one-half hours later, after six years preparation, he was distinguished as a world-famed aviator.

If we "work with marble, it will perish," but if we are true to that inner drive in bringing out the best; giving of ourselves, in adding joy to the environment we live in, we shall never be better employed.

"Water shapes itself to the vessel that contains it" and the soul of man limits itself to the measure of his thoughts. Thoughts of inspiration become the "open circuit" to greater rewards and blessings. What lies a head and what's left behind is of little significance compared to the potential of the mind; the power of understanding and riches yet to be developed within.

Uplifting words of creative thinking moves men to a high state of spiritual freedom, bringing joy to the heart. It's noiseless and never calls for loud laughter. A gracious thought comes with feelings; it's the voice of the soul that enhances the spirit; never talking back.

The effectiveness of kind words and lofty deeds mellows the heart in reaching people and bringing a oneness of understanding; revealing the more lasting promises.

It has been speculated by some inquiring minds, that in life following this, there will be restored to each the power to recall the things done in premortal experience; the things we did in the preparation for life on this planet earth.

When this unwritten chapter is added to or taken away from the total personality of our efforts, then we shall understand the value and need of preparedness. This life is the time for readiness for no other life can take its place. What we do to enhance the soul here becomes the supporting role to all that follows.

RULING POWER OF LIFE

As the clock strikes at the morning hour, it's more than a time of day, it's a time of duty, a time to grow...to reach out and become a more delightful and pleasure-giving person. Should we stumble and fall, it's paramount we arise and finish the race.

We, the people, make up the cast of characters of performing arts and skills on the world stage. Standing in the wings of premortal living are untold millions waiting for their turn on earth, waiting to audition and play their part here in this theatre of action. The makeup in this life is genuine, the costumes real, and the story lines unrehearsed. This drama is the premier performance of trial and error in the field of experience. A dedicated few receive a standing ovation.

It was Helen Keller who, at the age of eighteen months, had not only lost her sight, but she could neither hear nor speak. From the beginning, in the process of working her way through life, she came to know the world by touching it. The delicate feel of things became her voice of understanding and the channel through which came expressions and interchange of thoughts with her unseen world. It was the inner motivating power of love and determination to grow spiritually and intellectually that beautified her soul to a state of joy and happiness.

In this life of choice, we can reach for things big or small, with strength or in weakness, but we must keep seeking if we are to prevail and overcome. Miss Keller never quit gathering about her the greater riches in bringing maturity to living.

It's when the law of growth is rejected that we recede to a condition of self-distintegration, yet as we respond to talent and desire to overcome restrictions and difficulties, that's when we grow in substance, becoming more acceptable to the higher order of living.

All the things that are easy to do have been done years ago. Now is the time of new discoveries to challenge the seemingly impossible things. First and foremost is mastering the art of getting along with one another, and, secondly to exercise intelligence to the degree that when the Lord speaks, we all receive and understand the same message. We are yet to conquer and triumph over greed and selfishness that's so deadly to the soul. The gound of persistence must be cultivated where we now find ourselves if the gifts within are to be set free and the riches of the harvest gathered.

Theodore Roosevelt was continuous in the process of gathering knowledge and improving his intellectual capacity. He died with a book under his pillow.

There is need to recapture the purpose of this day for if we let a part of us die, it depresses that part which lives and we cut the thread of new beginnings and the hopes of a more satisfying life. It is good we attack this phase of living rather than merely define it, and with integrity of purpose be found in the safety zone of activity where the work may most effectively be done in reaching a state of perfection. Traveling down the center of the road is a poor place to be; that's where the white line is. . .it could be sudden death.

SEASONS

The seasons are the time clocks regulating the schedule in the life of man, animal, and all nature, revealing the hour to plant and the time to harvest. Nature speaks a language that all life understands.

Seasons forewarn the birds of their time to wing southward and summons them for the return flight. The bear is tipped off when to begin the long winter's nap and the hour it must awaken to seek a mate and perpetuate its kind. Man understands the signal telling him when to put on his overcoat and the time to take it off.

This universal clock covers all facets of living, for both those who work or play. Without the interval of seasons, life as we know it would be void and lose its meaning.

The wisdom and behavior of man is seen in the way he adjusts and fits into and accepts the law of nature, without which he could not exist. "There is a time to live and a time to die," but within this network of life are seasons of responsibilities to balance the scale of our allotted time against that which is required of us to do.

Our day on earth is but a moment of eternity to carry the torch in doing uplifting and enhancing things before the flame of opportunity goes out. Our dedication to living should be in design to complete the work at hand, building on the foundation that others so nobly left here for us to finish.

Everything good didn't happen yesterday. Today is laden with treasures of truth to be gathered from the passing stream of life so quietly flowing down the river of time, and the season is now to gather in the richness of the harvest.

Just as "darkness and light divides the course of time," each is spinning his or her own fate as they come face to face with the real thing; life itself, and the more we learn about the needs of our fellow associates the more we understand ourselves. And should we get upset with too much success too soon, life becomes complicated and out of context with things lovely and delightful and it is then the need arises to obey the warning signals at the crossroads of life, for on the freeway of living there are no stop signs that intercepts and halts the movements of time.

SIN

The role of evil is the "Master plan" of the Devil. It's a most devious and powerful scheme of corruption in outline to destroy all that is right and good in men.

Sin originates within the realm of the mind before launching out to gather in its own. Men determines the scope of its destructive force. Evil has no voice; we are its voice. It cannot see; we are the eyes. It has no power; we are the scope of its fury. It travels light; we carry the burden. It's without money; we "foot" the bill. It isn't self-sustaining; we sustain and become the platform from which it is launched.

Sin respects boundary lines; it never intrudes or invades the private lives of men without their consent. Satan delegated his power to Cain and he killed Abel.

Today evil is a vast movement thriving on the weakness of society. When lived it rules the hour; unlived, it dies on the vine.

The heart sets the rhythm and tempo of the soul. From this emergence of operation, life becomes rich in the history of little men becoming big through the quality of wealth and understanding drawn from the character of thought within.

In this competitive business of living, with its success and failures, man leaves his mark of choice witnessed in his works, knowing that back of everything that moves there is a force and back of every force there is a will, a power of determination. Back of this power of command there is a faith, the mainspring of the soul, and back of faith that moves men to greatness, there is God.

Man is a piece of the world with holdings in heaven and title to his belongings must be checked and established before residence can be taken up in the mansion prepared for him.

The function of happiness is the supreme business of living. It's a sound and vital part of our Father's business, of which he is concerned that we condition our personality for a state of celestial increase.

Sin is not on trial; it has been tried and condemned, yet it's alive. . .on the move. We alone keep it breathing to torment the soul.

SPLIT SECOND DECISION

In any field of endeavor the basic principle in attaining success is the clean-cut desire, coupled with determination to satisfy that inner drive to achieve.

In baseball few players make it to the big league without extensive training and aspiration to reach their goal. Baseball is an exciting sport. When the Umpire signals "play ball", the battle is on. The opening point of pressure is pitcher against batter. It's a contest of tension, intelligence, and skill, dealing in fraction of seconds. The game becomes a team effort where the players win or lose together.

A noted home-run hitter made an observation, stating that when a ball is hit dead-center, there is little chance of a "four-bagger." The most that can happen is a screaming line drive. To score a home run the ball must be hit slightly below dead-center.

Winning pitchers usually have five different speeds. The fast ball, traveling near the 90 mile per hour mark. A sinker pitch will do 85. A slider around 75 to 80 miles per hour. A curve ball will travel 60 MPH and a change-up pitch perhaps at 50.

The batter at the plate has a fraction of a second to interpret one of the five speeds as the ball leaves the pitcher's mound. If he fails to read the message, it's usually defeat at home plate. Unless the brain calculates the speed and rotation of the ball by the time it reaches the half-way mark, there's little chance for a hit.

On the playing field of life judgment takes place in the "now"...in split seconds. There isn't time for the final word of the last judgment. It isn't so much the nature of the deceptive pitch life throws, but that we are not deceived by what's coming.

Every successful failure insists that success is a matter of luck.

Our day of living on earth is a contest between the passing of time and a responsible life. It's the uncertainty of the "hit and miss" aspects of the game that adds suspense to the outcome. Desire, incentives and challenge keep the players on their toes. Only if the ball is hit over the fence can the batter take his time going around the bases.

A hard fought game is good to have over with, but not if it's the last game. Life is a long struggle that takes many years of work to become an "overnight" success.

Winning is easy to remember, while losing is hard to forget. The inability of making a hit everytime at the home plate of living, isn't failure. The real loss comes when one quits swinging.

We must prepare for the onslaughts of life in the training years. "Seeds falling on shallow ground bring prompt disaster."

STILL THEY ACCOMPLISHED

Napoleon during his march on Italy never saw the barrier of the Alps between his army and victory, and Washington who saw the Hessians at Trenton and chance for victory wasn't disturbed by the ice filled Delaware river. The boats were launched. Lincoln felt the spirit "of the people" and never permitted the leaders of a divided nation and the evils of slavery change his course. Edison saw the need of the storage battery, and failed to let ten thousand unworkable experiments tax his strength and deter his enthusiasm. Babe Ruth hit 714 home runs and paid little attention to 1330 times he struck out at bat. Brigham Young, the modern Moses, who came west to build an empire for man and a kingdom for God, never let the heat, dust and cold, the sick and dying blind him of responsibility.

The obstacles between the starting point and the goal, are the functions of living that brings out the best in men. Man is born to act and his failure to act places him in the realm of a spectator, standing in the wings on the world stage of life. It's the action of creative thought and ideas that bring overflow to living, enlarging the scope for a happy and fulfilling life. Creativity of beautiful things have no limitations in bringing joy to the heart of man. Life is an ongoing process made up of promising people everywhere seeking to discover and reaffirm the basic values for success in living.

It's through man's determined effort that he comes into his own. To succeed he must deliver. "Fame is merely the spirit of man that survives himself in the minds and thoughts of other men." Fame relates to a condition of successful living or a life misspent.

Behind thoughts we call our own are the ideas and efforts of many men. Those having the truth and riches of understanding must bear the responsibility of these gifts before the truth will set them free. Truth is where life begins. Without it life is lifeless. This business of living is a big operation; it's a life-time, a full-time job.

We see many uplifting things in others that we see only dimly in ourselves, yet we can never exhaust the resources within for so little has been tried.

The purpose of living is releasing the best we have in helping those in need. And should we find the door of opportunity to our Father's kingdom closed, it is we who have locked ourselves out.

SURPRISE FINISH

It was a midwinter day when a boy with unkempt hair and a dirty shirt wearing rickety shoes stood before Superintendent George F. Millikin, in the office of the Western Union and applied for work as a telegraph operator.

Mr. Millikin told the lad to come back at 5 o'clock and he would test his efficiency by having him take a message.

At the appointed hour young Tom Edison was there. In the meantime Mr. Millikin had arranged for the fastest telegraph operator in their New York office to send an 800 word news story by wire to his Boston office.

Young Mr. Edison gave the signal that he was ready. Faster and faster the dots and dashes came pouring in as he began writing and shifting papers. During the process members of the office employees gathered about to see how their planned scheme to trip up a country boy was working out. It was then that Edison knew it was a set-up. At that moment he opened his desk key and sent a message back to the New York operator with the words: "Come on

Mister, don't go to sleep on the job. Shake yourself and get busy with the other foot."

By then the office employees knew the "country boy" had caught on as to what the caper was all about and they rushed to the young man and showered him with congratulations.

This was a case where a young man early in life had prepared himself. He knew his job. He kept his composure and stood up under pressure. Dignity of youth was seen in action; he added quality to the day. He was seen as a person of responsibility; one of strength and character of purpose.

Mr. Edison succeeded on the front line of reality and gave an account. He knew of no other way than being true to his talents and the power of his potentials; putting back into his work a part of himself. One of his greater abilities was the power of control he had over himself. He considered the quality he wanted from life and paid the price to attain it, knowing that the harder the task the greater satisfaction in writing a finish to a job well done.

It's a matter of taste in the type of riches we want from life. A small thing well done is better than something half-done on a large scale.

To make time useful is to make it live and become alive in doing things uplifting for the joy of having done. "A thought can't be formulated without a thinker nor a plan without a planner."

SYMBOL OF COURAGE

A recent fire in an Idaho forest left many acres of blackened earth. A few weeks after the fire there was seen in full bloom a buttercup growing amid the burnt stubble. It stood alone shining through the blackness.

With no weeds to slow its growth it grew in beauty as a symbol of courage, of hope, of life; standing valiant and distinguished; challenging the sleeping plants beneath the dark soil to arise and put on their best dress and reach for a place in the sun. Even "Solomon in all his glory was not arrayed like one of these."

As we journey through life we see greatness in people who take a stand; remaining true to their convictions in doing what they know to be right. They live undauntedly in the present with faith in the future; standing erect, looking back occasionally only to see if the past has left a message. Within their hearts they get the feeling there's a "second chance" to rise again, revealing their best as the buttercup. Sometimes it takes the shadows of the darkest day to reveal and bring out the best there is to offer.

This is our time to extend spiritual boundaries and break new soil of understanding. The Lord has placed the germ of life in every seed of the field, and within the hearts of all men he has planted seeds of love for spiritual growth. Treasures are within reach to enrich life and when developed, it becomes the most powerful motivating influence for the good of man.

We are here to perpetuate our destiny. It was Florence Nightingale; too ill to move from her bed, who organized the hospitals of England. She became a shining light in the hearts of those needing her most.

It was Milton who wrote Paradise Lost after he was blind. He said: "Who best can suffer, best can do." Occasionally it takes trials to think difficult problems through to their solution. Problems sharpens spiritual perception with focus on things best suited for the soul. Being confined with yourself during difficult times, is sometimes the most profitable occasion one can spend in the presence of himself.

Illness gave Eugene O'Neill a second chance from a hospital bed. He began writing plays that revolutionized American drama.

Edison knew that the total voyage of life takes a life beyond this day when he said: "I've done my work; I've lived my life; and now I'm ready for the next job." Only on the freeway of mortality does life end here.

It isn't how tall in stature we stand, but it's how tall we are on the inside that brings satisfaction. Napoleon never liked himself as a person five feet two inches high, but he did the job best suited for his desires and drive.

We all have characteristics that can be enhanced with use. There is need to exercise the "do it now habit," and concentrate on growing things. The mind is a good take-off point. It has the potentials of keeping us young all over. We grow as long as we cultivate the spirit to good works. Among us are friends and associates who would give most anything for the gift of an untroubled mind.

As with the buttercup in its grandeur, this is a new day to make something good happen. From each of us the best is expected. It may be in the gift of bringing out the best in others.

TEACHER OF TEACHERS

Occassionally the castle we build in the sky isn't a fit place to live, yet within the heart, every dream house must have its beginning. A visionary individual is usually a thinker whose thoughts can't be put on "hold."

"One person blazes a trail; others build it into a highway." A newsboy named Edison lights up the world. A rail splitter, at one dollar a day, becomes President of USA. The first steamboat, telegraph and telephone; the reaper, the radio were in the beginning a dream in the mind of an individual.

E. H. Harriman dreamed of a railroad across the Great Salt Lake; it came true. Another dreamed of a tunnel under the Hudson river; it happened. The Wright Brothers visioned an airplane flying in space; footprints of man are recorded on the moon. "First the plan, then the broken ground, then the structures and the reality of a dream come true."

In the schoolroom of life, dreams are often interrupted by a commanding school teacher called "experience." This school master of experience calls for examination and demands answers to problems before questions are asked and the lessons studied.

Experience is a perpetual system of change; a trial and error method of learning; a function revealing how people react to head-on realities. Experience is a delightful but harsh taskmaster. Every encounter is designed as a test move revealing the best or worst in men.

The outcome of having come this way may not be a shining light, but the score identifies ones position of strength and puts a deep-freeze on what is written in the final chapter.

On the first day at school, there was a child who disliked the small chairs in the room. There was nothing to grow up to. His first impression was to challenge something beyond himself. He wanted progress, he wanted change, and most important he wanted recognition.

Experience is a continuous operation in the living present. It begins at birth and never quits. We reach a high order of living when we travel with sufficient humility while keeping the spirit manageable and hopes alive to challenge the events of new beginnings.

There is constant need of adaptability in meeting the problems of daily circumstances. Life's a dress rehearsal in preparation for the final exam at the Great Judgment. Divine gifts of the kingdom come only if we have prepared for their coming.

Bringing life into focus with reality and things spiritual is the greatest need of the hour.

THAT INNER DRIVE

It was Michelangelo who made the statement "He could see an angel in the rugged stone he was working on." He visualized and liberated beauty in bringing it to life, yielding to that inner drive of self-expression.

Some men dabble with life while others with perception and talent create masterpieces; the original of which others make copies.

Some manufactured articles today may be seen in the junk pile ten years from now, but products with imposing excellence of beauty and high quality, never find their way to the rubbish heap.

And it was Newton who discovered the law of gravitation before the age twenty-one. Unknowingly, however, he made one slight error in the measurement of the earth's circumference. Twenty years later he corrected his mistakes. The theory that planets roll in their orbits as a result of the same law that pulls an apple to the ground, was established as a fact.

"Millions say the apple fell, but Newton was the one to ask why."

Through the realm of thought and the drive to know, we learn of the world about us, and through reaching out comes a faith that the days a head will unfold with promise; but it's in the field of work and inspiration that awakens and challenges the spirit into action from which come the greater discoveries of life.

Truth was "on hold" waiting for Newton to discover it. Truth is lost only in ones failure to recognize it and man's capacity to accept truth makes justice possible, and having a perception of what is justice, makes truth necessary.

It's the unhealthy thought patterns that destroy moments of our usable time; adding up to wasted days.

It was columbus who unlocked the greatness of a new world, but equally important to challenge the spirit, were his words: "Sail on, sail on, sail on!"

"It's the set of the sail and not the gale" that determines the direction we take. Although birth begins the man, it's through obedience to law that sets him free.

It's better to keep the spirit clean and unbroken than pile up money and die fat and old and unloved in bed.

THE AMERICAN PROMISE

The most far reaching investment for highest returns is the total investment in the realm of righteous living. The Lord has promised that "unto the righteous," this land of America "shall be blessed forever more."

The fulfillment and destiny of this promising declaration is dependent upon the behavior of "we the people... the seal is set for our future. Preserving this nation and keeping it in good working order will take regenerated efforts of many builders in the role of loyalty and upright living. It calls for many carpenters to build, repair and maintain integrity of purpose. In the hearts of the people the spirit of Washington, Jefferson and Lincoln must prevail.

Evil ways isn't something new but our main concern with evil is that it's so successful and well organized in the work of disintergration and decay. It has been said: "All that is necessary to make evil triumph is for good men to do nothin."

The city of Ninevah, in its corruption, was saved because the people had a change of heart and repented while there was yet time. And there were the cities of Sodom and Gomorrah that were lost because less than ten worthy souls could be found.

"We, the people" have a heritage of freedom under God that is committed to our keeping. It's alive and real and by possession we must keep it breathing. Our founding fathers left their landmarks in giving us a free land to look after. We can't separate our sense of loyalty and allegiance as citizens, from the spirit of 1776. The fact we have our independence supersedes the reason for having it, yet to misuse freedom is to cheapen it, and to cheapen it is to lose it.

America is a land of liberation. . .not domination; coming to us as a right and function of trust, and its constitution is a document of action and with it comes the challenge of fulfilling the promises made by the Lord.

"Only an enlightened people can maintain the democratic process," and today the spotlight shines on America. We are a country with a known birthday that is remembered with significance by the people of every land.

THE BEGINNING

The earth's rotation on its axis is determined so accurately that a variation of one second in every one hundred years would upset the perfect order of law in the universe.

When did the earth have its beginning, when did time and life originate? Can you set a date? Every person is certain of having a beginning, but which beginning is he speaking of? One of body or spirit, mortal or premortal beginning?

The Lord in his precision calculations set up the element of time and space with perfect order and law designed for the blessing of man. Each passing day is a new birth of time, born out of eternity, and with its coming no one is here whose work is not born with him.

There is a tendency of being careless with the gift of years set aside for our span of living, yet goals must be reached within our allotted days. Time is controlled only by a better organized process of doing.

Out of the gifts of this century each of us have five and one-half horse power working for us—equivalent to forty slaves. Today we live better than the richest Greek or Roman who ever lived with all their workers. We have a surplus of time on our hands. According to Shakespeare "time will unmask falsehood and bring truth to us." The passing years stamp the seal of time in bringing truth to light in shaping the destiny of men.

We have been well advised in the things we must do to make the business of living more suitable for an exalted position. Although time runs a winning race, we must not lose faith in this trial run with those who have already come this way—who have gone before. We belong to them. They have experienced more in living than we, and their helping hand will be needed in the forward march ahead.

"In life the dancers dance and musicians play for them," and as the years pass time brings change while seasons continually move in to fulfill the law of the harvest— "As ye sow so shall ye reap." We have an overflow.

THE BEST YEARS

It was at the close of the day during October that a noisy Bluejay was eating lunch, in my back yard, from the head of a giant sunflower, while at the same moment there was a robin splashing itself clean in the birdbath, and overhead a flock of seagulls, whose chatter was loud and clear...calling attention to themselves, were in flight westward towards the Great Salt Lake. Being a lover of nature, caused me to reflect with fascination of the beauties so close to home; things waiting to be seen, to enjoy and admire.

To get the most from the passing years of time we should be mindful that the last hour of life will come in the present, and to receive the most from living, we must be alive to the gifts of each day; of things about us, for life to some has an ending before it begins, indicating that when we are called to a job of importance, the time for preparation is past; the sun has set, and failure to equip oneself... putting things in order during the training season, is forever gone and the reality of life reveals itself. The question arises, "has the best of life passed us by; have we lived the best years and accomplished our most effective work, or have we retired our potential and best efforts for the duration of mortality?"

As answers come, we may conclude if there is a plot of ground to till, plants to cultivate, flowers to pick, friends to visit, and music to free the soul, surely we live among promising years, and if there is joy in the beauty of the sunset, and the heart quickens with the laughter of children, and the echoing sound of a flashing stream stirs the wandering spirit within for a walk in the meadow, then the call of destiny has taken us by the hand. If uplifting thoughts, bringing joy to the soul, controls the hour while cultivating lofty ideals, then the feel of the more abundant life speaks to us out of the present. And if the fruit gathered from today's harvest is admissible for a place in our storehouse of our Father's kingdom, then the

best of life hasn't passed by, but has become apart of us...
traveling at our side.

THE COW WAS SOLD

There was a father who made the statement to his
friends that "he wished his boy," who was then working
for a large corporation, "would let down the bars and
drink with his business superiors, particularly on occasions of company parties." He felt it would be an opportune time for his son to move up much faster in the
company if he catered to their passing standards.

Here was a situation of father and son looking
through the same bars, the dad "saw the mud" and the
son, true to his convictions, "saw the stars."

Through unfounded examples, set by others, footprints of lost souls are tracked into eternity.

There was another parent who told his two young
sons that a man was coming to buy "Old Bess" the milk
cow. He cautioned his boys to act as if "Old Bess" was
their best milk producing cow and in the presence of the
buyer to try to persuade him their father, not to sell.

The man came on schedule, the boys did as they were
told and the cow was sold.

What the father told his sons on this and other
occasions was not to be their secret alone. Over the years
the echos of their unsound examples were heard and
made headlines throughout the state, spending several
years behind bars in various jails.

The law of intelligent growth insists that a good life can't be built out of bad examples.

Man is not a passing by-product of earth life. He's the real thing, a spiritual off-spring of God with claim for a place in the eternities, and while he is cast in the likeness and image of God, it becomes the Lord's main line of work to glorify and exalt man in bringing to pass the greatness of His glory.

Man's search for happiness is a movement of greatest concern. . .to find it is to find the light of truth, the gospel of Jesus Christ. Many things taken for truth are short-lived, becoming dissolved and obliterated under the pressures of time and circumstance. Those who lose the "straight and narrow" may find their way forward only by going back to the starting point where the principles of life and salvation have their beginning. Love and integrity of purpose are the portable items that we take with us and they become character witnesses in eternity upon which the fullness of life will evolve.

When attempted to do something wrong, and we look around to see if someone is watching, don't forget to look up.

THE COYOTE AND THE HARE

The running battle between the Coyote and the Hare has been going on through the ages. About 30 percent of the intake found in the stomach of the Coyote is meat from this animal. Running in an open field or up hill, the Hare will out distance its pursuer, but when two or more

Coyotes gets a rabbit moving in a circle, it may well be its last race.

The life expectancy of a rabbit, in Coyote country, depends on the direction it travels. Running in circles is suicidal to both man and animal in attempts to survive in this competitive world.

While touring Washington, D. C. a few years ago, we found the streets of the Capitol were laid out in a circle system. The map of the city indicated where important things were, but it didn't give the faintest idea how to get there. It seemed all roads led into the circle of traffic, but none leading out. We circled in confusion as the rabbit seeking an escape.

Life is made up of many diversions that clutters the mind in reaching out for happiness. And from the beginning, the time allotted to establish ourselves has never been free from shadows; for "into each life some rain must fall," yet today's heaviest burden is having nothing to lift. . .carry; nothing to be responsible for. We must earn the right to be here and return a part of ourselves for the gift of this day, for civilization is hard to come by. We must save the one we have even though there is need for some overhauling.

Vision the mighty oak. Time is the essence of its creation for putting on new wood in coming into its own. A moment of its usable time is never lost in moving upward to a boundless reach for the sky.

A leader of a world renowned choir said to his singers: "Do your best, that will be bad enough." Only the best is acceptable for growth in the kingdom of the Lord. Those doing less than their ability to do, cuts deep at the heart of becoming their best. A job half-finished never completely dies; but leaves the scar of the performers stamped on the bench-mark of the people.

Successful living is inseperably connected with the lives of men and women who with their inner-drive to accomplish, risk many falls to succeed but once while satisfaction comes in the "good works" of a job well done. It remains and speaks in silence as a gift of the giver.

The future never settles an issue until it makes contact with the present, while those moving in circles accelerate into obscurity at the same rate of speed as those who become satisfied and content with themselves. The story line of success belongs to the performer, not the observers; it relates to those moving with purpose in reaching out for a place in destiny. The earned blessings, predicated on the law of obedience, may be delayed in coming, but never denied for there is a lot of future out there waiting to see how this unrestricted gift of time is used.

THE ENTERPRISE OF LIVING

Life is big business; it's landscaped on a large canvas of operations. It's a going concern. A necessary segment of existence is allotted for the accumulation of things that add beauty to our day; uplifting values in the search of an abundance in living.

Earthly things are important, but they are not the most vital gifts of life. Regardless of how time is used, the most productive may not relate to the field of science, law, medicine, or other professions. The highest good comes in the performance of saving souls; the most important of which is saving our own. A most pressing need for happiness is building a way of life that reflects a likeness of our behavior to the ways of the Lord.

Centuries pass, generations come and go, civilization appears and disappears; blossoms and decays. Man in his desire to "be doing" has learned the know-how of making things happen, outlining courses in history that have become both smooth and turbulent.

It is evident that those who fail to acknowledge God as their Father can rarely stand the burden of themselves. They travel alone, lacking the intelligence of obedience to His laws and consequently fail to rise above the level of their own confused state. Some are content with what they have become, but all men must go through the season of trial and error before they can identify their position as men.

"Life is like a knife. We take it by the handle or the blade, depending on how we want life to serve us."

We are not here to be victimized by circumstances but to improve and overcome the course of events. . .ups and downs, and make something good happen, yet it is common knowledge that to be content with little is difficult but to be content with much is impossible. History leaves the message that great lives are ordinary lives lived with intensity. Regardless of conditions, this day is a time to stretch the mind with things good and uplifting; expanding the spirit for a happy and rewarding life. And we must have respect for the past and learn lessons from mistakes and recovery and be alert to explore new ideas with a touch of patience. . .for to crowd out the life of the spirit is discrimination that depresses soul to a condition where only we, with self determination contain the power to recondition and heal the wounds.

THE GATEWAY

Alexander the Great saw Diogenes looking at a parcel of bones, and he asked the Philosopher what he was looking for. He replied: "That which I cannot find, the difference between your father's bones and those of his slaves."

The power making up the element of "time" return the bones of all men to a common grave—the dust of the earth. In the beginning the earth was "cursed" for the sake of man...to dust he must return. In the setting of the grave, a King is no longer king, and a beggar no longer begs. Hearts cease to beat together; beautiful eyes lose their luster, and the faces of delightful people no longer glow. In the dust of the earth all men find themselves on the same level; unclassified where troubled souls find rest; patiently waiting for the dawn of a new day.

Jesus of Nazerath was born in a state of poverty. He grew in stature with divine power. His destiny was unrelated to wealth and worldly acclaim. He was conscious of power, but his greater strength was the power of restraint. Jesus lived with humility and died as a God, buried in a borrowed tomb. Having power of life over death, he revealed to all men that the grave is nothing except the gateway to all that is something—Eternal Life.

As we travel through life the only thing we need to believe is the truth; anything less is out of order and may be forgotten, for truth is illusion free, but it must be recognized; a half-truth is always the wrong half.

The most profound supporter of truth is "time." The greatest revealer of truth is the Holy Spirit and the number one enemy of truth is ignorance. The pretense of having knowledge never set anyone free.

With each passing day we either become better or worse; we never remain quite the same. Back of everything that moves is an unpredictable force, the success of which depends upon what is done within the dimension of time and space allotted. To live an eternity among scientists, it would be helpful to have a working knowledge of mathematical equations; if among musicians an appreciation of music would be most fitting, and to meet and dwell with the Lord, a prayerful study would best be made of his teachings and personality; knowing what He stands for and won't stand for.

Reverance for God is the beginning of wisdom and high quality living, and the nearer we live the principles he taught the more select company we become for ourselves.

THE GREATER LIFE

The Great Architect, during the process of organizing man and putting together all the working parts, fashioned a soul in His own likeness and image. We are his students in the field of learning, seeking to become a better people in binding the future to its promises.

Jesus, who was born of Virgin Mary, grew to maturity and bore record of His Father as He ministered among men. Through His atoning sacrifice the inhabitants of the earth become recipients of life beyond the grave; and that which is possible for us to be, the Savior has become; living in a state of perfection.

To reach the Lord in prayer, no appointment is necessary. He's on standby to meet the needs of His children. If we pray with sincerity of purpose, answers will unfold, line upon line and leaf by leaf. When we fail to acknowledge the Lord for His goodness, there comes a withdrawal of His light that depresses the spirit and parches the land, bringing a dry spell to the soul.

When the door of the kingdom is unlocked through the gift of prayer, we must give of ourselves in the performance of things useful. As we do things uplifting, the inner voice, the conscience, is always there telling us to "do more." Conscience is the voice of the soul that takes up residence at the early age of accountability. It never quits or goes away. It forecasts directions to take, bringing inner peace or frustration. It bites and it heals. One person will say that his conscience is "clear" while another declares it is "killing me."

The Lord has chosen to work through us for only with our consent are we received of Him. He is the light and truth that testified of Himself. He's the central figure, the "hammer and anvil" of life while we are the substance for the molding in the test tube of time.

We are aeons of time away from being perfected in body and spirit, and we alone lock ourselves out from the One who is perfected. If we seek things upright and beautiful our best years are not only before us, but the most promising days await us. The best is not passed even though a part is wasted seeking the lesser values ricocheted from the deception of men.

If we are enthusiastic and alive to the purpose and blessings of earth life, we are neither dying or wounded, but stand in readiness to seize the greater rewards of living that await us in the realm of things divine and never-ending.

THE MOON

The moon is a very deceptive piece of the Lord's creation. It's unproductive, an unfit place to live having no air to breathe or soil to till. When the moon is full, it's beautiful; yet so cold and barren, operating without a soul. It shines on reflected light, an intermittent glow borrowed from the lamp of the sun.

Unlike the moon, we are given the power and intelligence to fashion our own light, a light generated within. It's the light of the Holy Spirit, the light of Christ, designed for a continuous glow. There is no flow and discernment of truth we are more certain of than the truth revealed through the power and gift of the Holy Ghost, a gift that must be received and accepted with sincerity of purpose before its power shines through. Only when the acts of men are ratified by the Holy Spirit of Promise, will there come a light of understanding to the riches of eternal life.

We are not capable of living in this complex world without dealing first-hand with the creations of the

Creator. We are here because through right of choice we found it the best place to be. In the process of getting along with one another are those who delight in telling the Lord how to run his business, failing to remember that He set up the business of living and established the working rules in the beginning. The zero hour is a good place to start. . .confusion comes when we attempt to go back beyond the beginning point.

The story of our lives becomes a page that finds its way into the Book of Eternity. What we have written belongs to us, revealing our best or worst as we move to the measure of other men's thought. We are the channel through which the power of God forever moves. Our spirit relates to His power in the grand march through life which is but a day on the calendar of eternal life. We step to the tempo of hope and despair as the wheel of destiny charts it course toward a place of peace and happiness.

Failure to reach our goal is never so depressing as having no goal.

THE NEXT GENERATION

Good thoughts, worthy deeds, and words of inspiration often need repeating, retold and enlarged upon to be most effective. The basic truth about life cannot be too often repeated for with each sunrise a new crop of students enter the classroom of learning. We of the older generation need reminding that an old truth is a new and challenging truth to those hearing it for the first time.

We, the listeners, sometime become impatient as we hear speakers, through the years, relate the same character building stories and sermons on the topics of behavior; things we should do and not do, how to live a good and respectable life to gain a place of trust in the Kingdom of our Father.

Seneca has written: "A thing is never too often repeated which is never sufficiently learned." We learn from one another. Uplifting and character building thoughts must be passed along to each generation just as runners in a relay race pass the baton. It becomes a group effort. A team never wins unless the last man wins.

Montaigne has the statement: "I have brought along nothing of my own, except the thread that ties (another men's) thoughts together." One writer wrote that, "to select well among old things is almost equal to inventing new ones," and another said: "Quoting another author is the highest compliment you can pay to him." It was Emerson who made the statement that "Next to the Originator of a good sentence, is the first quoter of it."

Many writers will read in excess of a hundred volumes to get sufficient thoughts and ideas to produce one book. In this creative field authors need each other, and they look to each for help and inspiration. The power of one living word, set down in the right place, may be the key that enlivens a talent into new frontiers of thought.

Few writers are self-made. An author is merely the focal point through which others have contributed to his success, and in a sense of gratitude, is responsible to pass along his best works of inspiration for others to likewise feed upon.

Only as we improve in reaching out for the highly sought after values of living is the goal of success getting closer.

THE SEED OF LIFE AND DEATH

Among the variety of fruit trees growing in various parts of the world, there is one called the "Upas." The fruit from this tree, when eaten, is deadly poison.

When a branch of the Upas tree is grafted into and becomes a part of a life sustaining tree, the fruit from each branch is attractive and inviting. Both are delicious to the taste. The fruit eaten from one branch "kills" while the other sustains, yet both branches grow and receive their power to produce from the same source. The branches of the tree, while growing together in their cross purpose designs get along in the friendliest manner.

In the Garden of Eden there stood the "Tree of Life" and the "Tree of Knowledge of Good and Evil." The fruit from the "forbidden" tree was delicious to the taste and very desirable, yet within, it carried the elements of spiritual death.

When Adam and Eve ate of the fruit, they cut themselves off from the presence of the Lord; were cast out and henceforth placed into a fallen state of existence. They were locked in and dependent upon a Savior.

In their new environment on earth, however, there came a change. They were introduced to the " right of choice" knowing good from evil, receiving the agency to make decisions and hand-pick their destination.

There is a wide variety of fruit growing in the garden of mortal life waiting to be picked. The selection is unlimited and man is free to select that which seems to him the most desirable.

On the tree of daily living are grown the fruit of confusion, despair, and trouble. Also growing on the same tree are the fruit that carries the seeds of promise, unlocking the door to eternal life. Because some is delicious and other deceptive to the taste, man must be alert to that which is selected to sustain the journey. It may bring spiritual disintegration of the soul or a fullness of life...added upon.

The day is near when "all things will be restored to their proper order, everything to its natural frame..." We must not let the light of this day pass us by without building something good from it, for as long as there is something to contribute, we have never done quite enough. Our soul is perfected only as we perfect our actions, thoughts, and deeds.

THE SUN

The sun is the universal lamp giving light to the world; it's the fire that heats, the magnetic beam that guides and controls; feeding and sustaining all creations of the Creator. This ball of fire emits in one second more energy than has been used by man since civilization began.

This heavenly glow of light adds beauty to the cheeks of youth and color to the rainbow; spotlighting the earth in its rotation of night and day as it feeds the seasons of time.

With steadfastness and perfect order of operations, the earth records the circle of years that spells failures, recoveries and positions of strength.

Through the natural law of the creations, the earth tells its story and God speaks, and man must listen lest he becomes a "wanderer in a strange land;" losing the incentive to reach out for the blessings of the more abundant life.

". . .every man walketh in his own way, and after the image of his own god, whose image is in the likeness of the world." A worldly image is counterfeit and unacceptable to the elect program of the Lord. The ways of the world are deceptive. Man in confusion indicts and cuts himself off from the soure of greater riches. Many men and women travel with a doctor's degree in education and a third grade command of thought and behavior in the field of higher learning. Being misinformed of the higher values pertaining to life eternal, people rob themselves of the truth about themselves and lose their identity in relating to God.

The talents of men become imprisoned by their failure in responding to the voice of the spirit. The greater loss comes, however, when we adjust to our own weakness rather than reaching for the higher order of performance designed for a healing and restoration.

Everyone has the built-in safety-valve called the "conscience." It's a guiding light, and alive to the need of bringing happiness to the heart within the bounds of a satisfying life.

Overcoming spiritual blockades unlocks the door of opportunity so basic in reaching a fullness of living. It's the glow of beauty and charm acceptable to the Lord's outlined way of life.

Prayer is a vital link to that inexhaustible power of God, a force that spins this great ball of dust called earth of which we belong and are a part.

THE TEMPEST WITHIN

It was about twenty centuries ago that the Savior and his diciples went out to sea. A storm arose while the Savior slept, but he was awakened as the words were spoken: ". . .carest thou not that we perish?" "Lord save us."

This was not the first nor the last time this question has been asked. In this world of conflicts, disease and sorrow, many people have reached the breaking point and have pondered the question in their hearts: "Lord, carest thou not that we perish."

Jesus calmed the sea but other storms have continued their course. The most destructive storms, however, are not the storms of the sea. The most violent are the tempests originating within the hearts of men.

We have air condition for the home and refrigeration to cool the milk, but where is the mechanical devise that cools the tempers of men?

The Lord holds the key to control the passions and contentions among men. He has given us a day of the Sabbath to keep us from doing any worse. He is the starting point. Unless we start with him, we begin at no fixed point and work to no end. He is reached only as we qualify to do business in his name. It takes special training to become an expert in the Lord's outlined work plan. If we seek sincerely, he will hear and restore, bringing purpose to living without wounding the heart.

We cannot be represented at the Great Judgment by delegate; we must be there in person. There are some things that can't be delegated to others. Jesus didn't ask Peter to use the whip cord to drive money changers from the temple. He never asked James to wash the feet of the disciples, nor John to fast forty days and nights. Nathaniel was never asked to carry the cross, nor Judas to bear the crown of thorns. The suggestion was never made to the Apostles that lots be cast to see who would die for Him. He knew the worth of the soul; and through his Atoning Sacrifice left the most challenging message, "Follow Me." This we must do successfully if we are to move into the realm of life eternal.

THE TEST

Baseball scouts on the lookout for new prospective pitchers seldom make up their minds about new players until they are seen in action—in the process of winning or losing. Recruiters are concerned how young players do under stress. . .when the pressure is on in the thick of battle;, giving attention to the way they perform in various situations. Will they crumble or remain stable and collected when things are not going well? Are they emotionally strong? Do they hold up under "fire?". . .The score in lights mean little.

The established rule in the game of life encompasses a trial run, a checking up process of the contestants while on the playing field. During action, as men compete against men, there comes into view a wide variety of frustrating moments in their search for affluence and well being. At times when it appears victory is won and a project finished, someone has come along and built a "better mousetrap," revealing that while you took a day off, he was on overtime.

A runner may be guaranteed to win the race only if there is no second entry, but those bringing useful changes into the lives of others are all winners.

The challenge in life is to keep a fighting spirit; retaining courage and determination to "pitch" with more finesse within the strike zone of a winner. It's when we fail to let our mistakes and miscalculations teach their lessons that we become lost and out of reach to the riches of living.

Each player in the business of living must be coachable and teachable in bringing to the surface the gifts of stability and balance for the more abundant life. To do this man must first find himself to become himself for this is the law upon which life is penetrated. Only then will he zero in and release to the world the waiting gifts at his command.

William G. Jordon said: "Today is all we have left to assert all that is best in us and today is the only time left to conquer the worst in us."

THEY DID IT

When it is said a thing can't be done and we do it anyway, it brings an inner joy; adding zest to living.

Columbus was considered foolish believing he could open the way to the east by going west. But he did it.

A young lad of 15, Joseph Smith, was confused to the point of believing he could inquire of the Lord in prayer and know which church to join. His answer came.

George Washington was indifferent to the point of supposing he could cross an ice filled Delaware river, at night, in a snow storm, and conquer the Hessians at Trenton. He accomplished the job.

Marconi, the Italian inventor, was considered "stupid" to believe he could send an electrical current through solid substance. It came about and wireless telegraph was born.

George Westinghouse was contrary to the point in believing he could stop fast moving trains by using air pressure. Trains are stopped today by this method.

Most difficulties we face in life are not in things, but about things. We often use the excuse, I'm too old, I started late, I haven't sufficient know-how.

Ideas about things need re-evaluation. The word "I can't" is overworked and should be put to rest. It isn't a fact, "It's an opinion." It's an idea borrowed that is deceptive. It should be swapped for the better idea, "I can." This life is written in the constitution of facts and figures. "I can't" is unreal and should be nailed to the floor.

A most delightful way of renewing the spirit and enhancing the soul is to descend from the mountain top of our pride, go straight, keep right, and dwell among the people. It's fertile ground for spiritual growth where seeds of understanding are planted and the harvest gathered.

Some flowers have only a few days in the sun and they begin to wither and fade. Other plants, with special qualities, are the evergreens. They stay with us the year around, taking the best of the winter blast. By the very nature of our creation we have the capabilities of being the evergreens, standing erect under stress regardless of things thrown our way.

With spiritual self-reliance we can be the light of the world for others to follow. This we must do; we can if we choose.

TO BECOME A CHILD

The Lord made it plain he was concerned with the underprivileged people of the earth when he said: "Inasmuch as ye have done it unto the least of these, ye have done it unto me," and there was concern about the over-privilege in his words: "For what man is profited if he gains the whole world and loses his own soul?"

There is need for consistency of balance between the extremes of "too much and too little." The gifts of the Kingdom are within the reach of all who desire to better themselves in seeking a place of residence with the Lord. The length of years cannot be pre-determined, but we have within the power to measure the quality and scope of this day in becoming a better and more delightful person.

The passing years, with blunders and restoration, coupled with wisdom and understanding of the more basic things to living, have a unique way of seeking their own level; defrosting the spirit and mellowing the soul to a place of trust in the business of getting along with one another.

As a child looks up to his father, hoping to become a person as he, a father, after having been crushed, entrapped and renewed from the challenge of daily struggle, often looks to the hour when his heart will mellow and with promise become as a little child. In that

moment he discovers where the higher values are and
detects the need of attaching himself to things lasting, to
something that grows and moves up beyond the perishable things of this elusive existence.

On this short-lived excursion there is constant need
in reaching out with an expression of love in helping the
under-privilege. There is need for stability of action and a
daily infusion of the higher values that come from the
uplifting thoughts and kind acts. Selecting treasures to
enrich the day, unlocking the door of peace and contentment to the evening hour, makes up the force of living.

We didn't come this way to be a sentinel, to merely
stand guard. Life calls for something more fulfilling. A
photographer, at times, slows down the lense of his
camera to let more light in. . .to get a more satisfying
picture. It's called "time-lapse" photography. And there
is need that we contain a testimony of the spirit, letting
more light of understanding penetrate our being for a
blending and mellowing of the soul.

"TO THINE OWNSELF BE TRUE"

Mr. K. V. Kaltenborn, a famous broadcaster wrote:
"After fifty years as a reporter, I hadn't always been
right, but I remained true to myself, reporting events I
considered important regardless of cost or consequence. I
never let public opinion undermine my integrity of
thought and courage to say it. The statement: '. . .to thine
ownself be true and thou canst be false to any men,' was
my guideline."

There is a time to live and a time to die, but this day of life is the hour to be true to oneself. Being true to self creates a beautiful environment that stays with us wherever we go. We must not settle for a "place in the sun" for anything less than the person we are. It is then we travel with a newness of heart, picking choice fruit from the garden of life.

If the course we take be pure; our actions good and right, we can safely get on with the business of living. There are no laws in heaven upon which blessings are predicated for commandments unlived.

To keep our identity alive and well, we must be true to the purpose for which we are here. Even a spoken "word" must remain true to character and put in the right place at the right time to generate power and live and become pointed and effective in its meaning. Through the centuries the product "salt" has remained true to itself, true to character and purpose, never losing the unseen power of its savor for the needs of man. It has never been false to the service it was created to give.

This land we live in called "America" was born to its greatness and intent when it awakened and became true to its beginning. The integrity of this people arrived when the majority of its citizens could no longer tolerate the blight of slavery. The day the slaves were freed was the hour of destiny for a stronger America. The effectiveness and strength of a nation tomorrow can never be higher than the integrity of its people today.

We can take from this day what we will, but we must be selective in choice; a price tag is attached. If that which is added to the storehouse of holdings fail to measure up to something we can be happy with, we've then paid a price much too high for our coming this way.

TOO MUCH

In the world of economics too much of something or the oversupply of a certain commodity becomes a vital concern in the law of supply and demand. Too much reduces the value of a product. The item itself, although high in quality, becomes less sought after and often downgraded because of an abundance.

This planet earth has waited untold centuries for you and me to come along and become a part of its going business. There are experts, however, who become alarmed and concerned that there are too many of us...an oversupply; that the physical makeup of the world is without capacity to feed and sustain the guests coming this way. Those having concern for an "Overpopulated" world have a tendency to cheapen the right to be born, placing the soul of man below par, beneath the level of material values.

Regardless of conditions and poverty stricken circumstances in which a person is born, his or her life should never be considered worthless and without claim to the gifts of their day. No one should be called "worthless for whom Christ died."

Born in Naples, Italy, was the 19th child of a family of 20 boys. An oversupply for one family it would appear. He was a runt of a kid, yet Enrico Caruso, today, is considered among the world's great singers of the past.

Everyone, regardless of quality of performance or length of days, adds to and becomes a single and vital sentence to the manuscript of life; a page that can't be separated nor omitted. Each life is a part of the main text. Every person born is a potential leader in training who has a past with a challenging future. The likeness to our Father in Heaven is within each to reveal its closeness. The undeveloped butterfly is alive within the caterpillar.

The gracious people of the earth are those who lighten the overload of their fellow associates; never adding the sting of their judgment to the burdens they carry. Lifting the spirit of one who is downcast and discouraged; making him feel needed and accepted is likened to the spirit of a "forgiving father" who "killed the fatted calf" for the wayward son who returned with a repentant heart.

It was William G. Jordon who said: "Often when we think we are studying the character traits of a person, we are only observing his outward characteristics. We learn only a part of another's character, for we see only the depths to which he may sink, but never the heights to which he may rise.

In passing this way, "man takes ore, stone, clay and builds beautiful structures that become works of art, but the greatest and most lasting masterpiece he will leave to his family and associates will be that which he does with the clay that bears his name."

TURNING POINT

It has been written that one of the great scenes in American History unfolded on April 5, 1621, as the Mayflower was bobbing at anchor in the little harbor at Plymouth. This small ship was ready to sail back to

England. The winter in America had been bitter. Death
had cut deep. Of the original 102 Pilgrims who came
seeking a life of choice and freedom, fifty survived;
twenty-one men and six lads. . .the rest were women and
children. Destiny was at work.

When the captain on the Mayflower extended the
final invitation to those on shore to return to their
homeland where they could enjoy a place of comfort and
security, not one accepted. Fifty people who might have
given up their quest for freedom said "no" as they
watched the ship become smaller and smaller as it sailed
away. They ignored guarantees and security and stayed
true to the voice within. Love of freedom was stronger
than death; their spirit and determination became the
spirit upon which America had its beginning.

When the empty ship sailed from the shores of this
land, it became a significant date in the history of
America. Since that point in time, people have come from
every spot on earth. . .to stay, never going back.

The Mayflower brought seed, not a harvest. The
seeds grew in the rich soil of independence and produced a
nation "of the people. . .by the people" for the blessing of
mankind.

When the great ship, Queen Mary, is forgotten, the
Mayflower will continue to sail its course in the hearts of
men the world over.

It isn't having an abundance of material things that
makes a nation rich, it's the capacity and ingenuity of the
poeple who produce that bring riches. Wealth isn't in
things; it's on deposit in the hearts of people who do
things. It is using the power of restraint in wisdom that
frees the spirit and reinforces the soul.

Those coming to America sought security of the land and freedom of choice. They built cities, factories and conquered the soil making it the most productive place on earth. Today this country that is "marked for plunder" by some nations, remains a land of choice and continues to challenge the unchained spirits of men. Self-determination is alive in America and dwells within the heart of a self-governing people.

VALUES

A sick child is never taken to the hospital and asked to be given two-hundred dollars worth of medical care. The answer is, "save my child." The price tag of survival hasn't been calculated on the scale of spiritual values. Nor is a child taken to school with the request of giving it two-hundred dollars worth of education. The cost of education reaches beyond the value of money on deposit. It's a debt the present generation is responsible for and must pay to stabilize the behavior and education of their replacements. The high price paid for the lack of education, reveals itself on the scale of ignorance and lack of understanding.

Some of the best educated people are those who snatch a few scraps of learning during the hours and intervals of time while rearing families and making a living. Being destitute of knowledge pertaining to the basic things that brings joy to living, demoralizes the spirit and muddles the significance for which we are here. To depress and dismantle the hopes of man is the motivating force of the Devil. It's a work he is skilled in bringing to pass. There are no diminishing returns from the blessing received through obedience to the laws upon which blessings of the kingdom are predicated.

Education is a two-fold program, designed for the "now" and "forever." This life is the time; it's postmarked "today." No one can withstand its march. Once the postmark of a day having been lived is stamped, it becomes the seal of a "yesterday," and time ratifies and validates it for evermore.

Only as we rely on our own experience do we get a limited education, and by the time we graduate from the schoolroom of mistakes and recoveries we are too time-weary and used up to go to work.

The best test in the application of a true education is in what we do with our leisure time. There are many pleasant things we do here that will be disallowed in the next working phase of life. To make this trip more enjoyable we must hold on to and grow with that which enriches the soul.

As we give, while we are here to give, it fulfills the greater law. It isn't so much how long we live, but what we do while it lasts.

Only with dignity of understanding to the purpose of coming here do we tie the future into the present, making eternity a part of today. Once this journey is launched there is no turning back. There is, however, an unlimited space ahead designed for open field running to challenge the best for the highest returns.

WE ARE INDEBTED

During a storm a young man's sailboat capsized and he fell overboard. He swam toward shore and as he neared the bank, fifty yards away, he panicked and began fighting the waves. It appeared he wouldn't make the distance when a man standing on the edge, who knew the nature of the terain beneath the water, shouted: "Hey, Mister, put your feet down!" The young man got the message and lowered his feet. The water came to his midsection as he walked to safety.

In a few feet of water this person may have drowned, but he listened and in a crisis heard the voice that directed his course.

That which we are and become, we owe to someone standing at the living edge of life. As we get the feel of the spiritual terrain encircled about us, we "never stand alone;" standing near are those who care. "Goodness is the only investment that never fails." The things we do for ourselves die with us; but doing good in helping those in need, remain on course as an arrow in its flight through space.

To attain success in living is contingent on the values of the things we do first. Some actions have preeminence over others. The Lord said: "Seek ye first the kingdom of God. . ." Doing second best in the Lord's work isn't good enough. Fruit grown on the tree of obedience is the first fruits of intelligent life before the celestial harvest comes.

In the process of learning we crawl before we stand and walk before running. A life saving principle is learning to float before swimming. Doing the right things first is a spark of refined wisdom, unlocking new horizons in reaching out for the greater gifts of things spiritual.

Indepth things of promise come at the price of effort. Many of the selected treasures we gather along the way, are not "home free"....they are subject to the test of time. This day is not only the hour to endure but the time to prevail in seeking the shoreline of safety for a happy and fulfilling life.

To have read a book by the open fire while the crackling sound of burning wood fills the air, is knowing what the quality of contentment is. Holding your new born child for the first time comes the feeling of what the rewards of family is. And having been a part of both is the rich discovery of what the gift of wealth is.

As we add quality living to this day; tomorrow will come bearing the greater riches of things lasting.

WHICH ROAD

Sometime ago, with an adventurous spirit, I went to one of the surrounding canyons for the purpose of hiking, exploring and inhaling the beauties of nature. It was most fulfilling to see and feel the glory of the Lord's handiwork.

Coming to a fork among the little used trails, I was faced with a decision as to which path I should take. Stopping to reflect, I ask myself the question: "If I take the one to the left, where will it lead? Will I lose my bearing and landmark and become lost, or will it lead to greater heights where I may look beyond the trees and see the valley below?"

During the span of living, all men must make the decision: "Which road shall I take, where will it lead, where will it end?" The end of a story will have recorded many new beginnings. Each step up the mountainside gives a better range of vision between the earth and the sky, but to receive the greater riches, one must return to the valley and dwell among the people. Too much time is often spent reaching the mountain top of our desires, only to find that the soil is unproductive and can't be cultivated when it is reached.

We have traveled the wrong road if the state of our presence here has failed to make a difference to others in helping them along the way.

Slowly we climb toward the distant mountain of time to record our final hour in the setting sun, and as the required course is traveled, the most important thing to be claimed as our own, will be a knowledge and understanding that God lives and Jesus is the Christ. Sharing a knowledge of things good and uplifting, divides and multiplies itself into the hearts of others, bringing joy to many.

While teaching the multitude in the desert, word came to Jesus that it was past noontime and there wasn't food sufficient to feed the people. He didn't ask the leaders to count the people. . .Count the loaves! "How many loaves have ye?" Jesus was in control and the five loaves and a few fishes multiplied with their use and thousands were fed.

We are not here to count our blessings but to bring blessings into the lives of others, nor are we here to suppress talents but to use our capabilities in putting talents to greater use. The spiritual capacity of man increases to the degree it brings into the lives of others, useful changes that enhances the soul.

We are not here to calculate the handicaps of life but to reinforce the riches of the kingdom. It's a personal project. . .for unless we succeed alone we shall never enjoy success together.